FRANCIS NGANNOU

The Journey from Poverty to Heavyweight Champion

Alexander V. Zeller

Copyright © 2024 by Alexander V. Zeller

All rights reserved. No part of this publication may be reproduced, distributed, or transmitted in any form or by any means, including photocopying, recording, or other electronic or mechanical methods, without the prior written permission of the publisher, except in the case of brief quotations embodied in critical reviews and certain other noncommercial uses permitted by copyright law.

Table of Contents

Introduction
Chapter 1: Journey of a Champion
    Early Life in Cameroon
    Childhood and Upbringing
    Struggles in Poverty
    Dreaming of a Better Future
Chapter 2: The Journey to Europe
    Escaping Cameroon
    Harsh Realities of Migrant Life
    Homelessness and Perseverance in Paris
Chapter 3: Discovering MMA
    Introduction to Martial Arts
    First Steps in the MMA World
    Early Training and Challenges
Chapter 4: Rise in the UFC
    Debut Fights
    Gaining Recognition
    The Knockout Artist
Chapter 5: Becoming UFC Heavyweight Champion
    The First Title Shot
    The Road to the Championship
    Victory and Becoming the Heavyweight

>King

Chapter 6: Fighting Style and Training
>Physical Attributes and Strength
>Key Techniques and Knockouts
>Training Regimen and Work Ethic

Chapter 7: Challenges and Setbacks
>Losses and Learning Experiences
>Overcoming Personal and Professional Obstacles

Chapter 8: Life Outside the Octagon
>Humanitarian Efforts
>Motivational Speeches and Public Appearances
>Role Model and Inspiration

Chapter 9: Legacy and Future Prospects
>What's Next for Francis Ngannou
>His Impact on the MMA World

Conclusion

Introduction

A name that appeals to supporters and prospective athletes alike is Francis Ngannou. Ngannou, born in Batié, Cameroon, on September 5, 1986, is a man whose rise from the streets of his hometown to the top of the mixed martial arts (MMA) scene is truly remarkable. Being renowned for his explosive strength and unwavering resolve, he has established himself as one of the most formidable heavyweight fighters in UFC history.Ngannou faced hardships in his early years. As a child living in extreme poverty, he encountered many obstacles, which helped him mold his personality and ignite his passion. He moved to France to follow his aspirations, but soon after, he was broke and without money. But he persevered and loved fighting sports, so he started training in boxing and mixed martial arts (MMA), where he found his innate striking ability.Ngannou started his incredible ascent in 2015 when he made his professional MMA debut. He established himself as one of the sport's fiercest hitters by showcasing his amazing knockout power in every fight. In addition to making him the UFC Heavyweight Champion, his victory over Stipe Miocic in March 2021 also established his place as a major career achievement and global sports icon.

Beyond his accomplishments within the octagon, Ngannou is a supporter of empowerment and social change. Through his platform, he encourages people to follow their aspirations no matter what, especially those from disadvantaged backgrounds. This book explores Francis Ngannou's life and career, including his setbacks, victories, and legacy both inside and outside of the mixed martial arts community. Come along with us as we explore the life of a champion who personifies the real meaning of tenacity and resolve.

Chapter 1: Journey of a Champion

The incredible story of Francis Ngannou's ascent to the top is one of tenacity, willpower, and the unwavering pursuit of ambitions. His tale starts in Batié, Cameroon, where he encountered several challenges that would influence his course in life. Ngannou was born into a family that was experiencing financial hardship, therefore his early years were difficult. He saw firsthand the hardships his village faced as a child and learned early on the value of grit and diligence.

Inspired by the renowned Mike Tyson, Ngannou took an interest in boxing at the age of twelve. It was difficult for him to follow this desire, though, as Cameroon lacked training facilities and resources, forcing him to learn on the go. He was still committed to getting well despite these setbacks. He took the risky decision to leave Cameroon at the age of 26 in order to pursue his goal of becoming a professional fighter in Europe.

When Ngannou got to France, he was met with harsh realities. He ended up homeless and was on his own, fighting for survival in a strange nation. But it was in these trying circumstances that he found his real purpose in life. He started off by honing his boxing and mixed martial arts (MMA) techniques at a nearby gym. With the help of knowledgeable trainers, Ngannou's undeveloped skills started to blossom.

He made his professional MMA debut in 2015, and the fighting community took notice of him right away. His distinct fighting technique and powerful knockout power made him stand out from the competition. He advanced through the ranks with every battle, displaying his extraordinary strength and willpower. Ngannou rose quickly in the UFC, where he was respected by both fighters and spectators for his vicious knockouts and earned performance bonuses.

When Ngannou competed against Stipe Miocic for the UFC Heavyweight Championship in March 2021, it was the apex of his career. Years of devotion and hard work culminated in the fight. Ngannou proved his devastating power in a match that will never be forgotten, finishing Miocic and taking the title. This triumph demonstrated his rise from modest beginnings to championship success and cemented his place as one of the most feared heavyweights in MMA history.

Ngannou is dedicated to encouraging people and giving back to his community outside of the octagon. Using his position, he promotes social change by stressing the value of tenacity and the conviction that anybody can realize their goals, no matter what obstacles they face. His story serves as a potent reminder that anyone can triumph against adversity if they have perseverance, hard effort, and an unwavering spirit.

The life of Francis Ngannou is a monument to the strength of the human spirit and dreams.

He is still an inspiration to many as he forges ahead as a champion, demonstrating that success is attainable for those who are prepared to put in the necessary effort.

Early Life in Cameroon

On September 5, 1986, Francis Ngannou was born in the Cameroonian town of Batié. Ngannou was raised in an impoverished and resource-poor area, and the difficulties he faced as a child molded his goals and character. Being the child of a street fighter for a father and a multitasking mother, he experienced directly the hardships faced by his family and neighborhood.

Inspired by his love of boxing and the anecdotes of sports legends, Ngannou dreamed of being a professional athlete from a young age. He started pursuing this interest at the age of 12 by impromptu boxing training using whatever equipment he could find. Regretfully, realizing his goals proved to be challenging in a nation where coaching and training facilities were hard to come by.

Despite all of these obstacles, Ngannou never wavered in her resolve. He was drawn to the neighborhood gyms frequently so he could watch and pick up tips from seasoned boxers. But it was hard to train regularly or take part in official tournaments without financial backing. His difficult background gave him a strong work ethic and an unwavering will to do better.

When Ngannou became 26 years old, his life changed drastically. He took the brave decision to leave his home and pursue a better life in Europe after realizing the restricted options accessible to him in Cameroon. This was more than just chasing aspirations; it was a struggle for success and survival in a world where everything seemed to be against him. Ngannou set off on a treacherous voyage that would finally bring him to the borders of France, leaving behind everything he knew.

His formative years in Cameroon established the groundwork for his success as a champion.

Adversity taught him resilience, fortitude, and the power of determination, and those teachings were the cornerstones upon which his career was constructed. These memories would continue to orient him while he navigated the difficulties of his new life in France, serving as a constant reminder of his origins and the obstacles he had surmounted.

Childhood and Upbringing

Francis Ngannou's temperament and aspirations were greatly influenced by his difficult yet resilient childhood and upbringing in Batié, Cameroon. He was raised in a humble household and was exposed to the hardships of poverty at a young age. His mother, who worked multiple jobs to support the family, and his street fighter father instilled in him a strong work ethic and perseverance.

Ngannou was surrounded by the hardships of living in a developing nation while growing up in a rural area. Despite having limited access to resources and knowledge, he showed a strong desire to study and an insatiable curiosity. He was always interested in sports as a kid, especially boxing, because of the great competitors he watched on TV. He trained informally, often with friends and innovating with homemade equipment, despite the absence of training facilities and funding.

Ngannou faced emotional and psychological difficulties in addition to physical hardships during his upbringing. He had to deal with the constraints of his surroundings, which were sometimes depressing. But instead of letting these challenges define him, Ngannou came to have a clear sense of purpose. He discovered how to focus his frustrations and goals into his training, making the most of every obstacle to further pursue his goals.

He had his first taste of fighting at the age of twelve when he began to compete in neighborhood boxing fights. These early encounters had a significant influence on his fighting technique and mental toughness. He grew to have a great respect for the sport after realizing that it provided a means of escaping the limitations of his childhood and a route to a better life.

Despite his hardships, Ngannou had many happy memories of his early years spent with friends and family. He gained an appreciation for the ideals of support and community, which he would carry with him throughout his life. His desire to achieve was fuelled by the link he had with his peers—peers who also aspired to be successful in sports.

Ngannou's desire to pursue a career in fighting intensified as he got closer to adulthood. Nonetheless, he made a crucial choice after realizing there weren't many options in Cameroon. He left his native country at the age of 26 in pursuit of better opportunities, which helped him go from a little child who wanted to box to a well-known mixed martial artist.

Ngannou's early life and upbringing gave him the resiliency and willpower that would come to define his professional life. Every obstacle he overcame aided in his development and gave him the mental toughness required to succeed in the difficult world of professional boxing. His rise from the backroads of Batié to the international scene is a stirring example of how one's upbringing should not limit their potential.

Struggles in Poverty

Francis Ngannou's early life in Cameroon was marked by extreme poverty, which had a lasting impact on his path. He was raised in Batié, where he was exposed to the harsh realities of living in a developing nation where it was frequently difficult to obtain essentials. His family suffered greatly from financial instability and battled to make ends meet. This setting shaped Ngannou's mentality and goals by instilling in him a deep sense of adversity and survival.

Due to a lack of resources, there were significant restrictions on access to training and education. Ngannou's early-ignited love for boxing faded as he dealt with the hardships of poverty daily. He was forced to rely on his imagination and willpower to follow his hobbies because there were no formal coaching programs or training facilities available. He would frequently work on his boxing skills alone, utilizing improvised gear and sparring with like-minded friends.

Ngannou saw his parents' problems directly as a child. His mother worked multiple jobs to maintain the family, while his father earned a pitiful salary as a street fighter. Their difficult family life was characterized by uncertainty and struggle as a result of their financial strain. Despite these challenges, his parents taught him valuable lessons about the importance of patience, hard effort, and having faith in oneself to overcome one's circumstances.

Ngannou's desire to get out of his predicament was fuelled by his encounters with poverty. He considered sports as a way to better his family's lives and a possible channel for change. But the trip wasn't without its challenges. He often felt burdened by the expectations of society and worried about the future most evenings. Dreams felt like an uphill struggle, but he wasn't going to let hopelessness rule his actions.

The pivotal moment occurred when, at the age of 26, he decided to leave Cameroon in pursuit of greater possibilities in Europe. This was a decision based on survival and self-improvement, not just a desire to become a professional fighter. Ngannou's courage to take chances to achieve his goals was a reflection of his early-life resilience.

Rather than defining him, his experiences as a poor child served as the cornerstone on which he constructed his future. They gave him a strong sense of direction and a ferocious will to succeed. Through his experiences, Ngannou developed his fighting technique and mental tenacity, which have given him the tools he needs to overcome obstacles in his professional career. He took the teachings of his upbringing with him as he made the journey from the dark shadows of his past to the brilliant lights of the fighting arena, serving as a constant reminder to himself and others that it is possible to rise above adversity and achieve greatness.

Dreaming of a Better Future

In the middle of his poverty troubles, Francis Ngannou harbored a persistent desire for a brighter future. He dreamed of a life beyond his circumstances from a young age, one in which he could improve his family and community in addition to escaping the struggles of his early years. This dream turned into a motivating factor that saw him through hardship and kindled a ferocious will to succeed.

Ngannou, who was raised in Batié, frequently turned to sports, especially boxing, for comfort. He felt inspired by the pictures of legendary warriors and their victories and accomplishments. He pictured himself winning the success that had escaped him in his regular life by displaying his skill and strength in the ring. This vision was entwined with his desire to inspire everyone around him and give his family a better life, not just for himself.

Ngannou's aspirations stemmed from a deep comprehension of the difficulties his people faced. He aspired to be a ray of hope for others and end the poverty cycle that held so many people captive. He felt that if he was successful, he could assist others overcome their hardships and open the door for upcoming generations. His desires were fuelled by this selfless motivation, which inspired him to work diligently towards his objectives.

Ngannou remained resolute in his pursuit of his goals despite training informally, practicing boxing with friends, and depending on ingenuity. With every strike of the fist and every drop of perspiration, he got one step closer to fulfilling his dream. Every setback taught him something new, and he used that knowledge to drive his unwavering quest for a better life. His will to make his ambitions come true and his confidence in himself both increased.

Ngannou took the decisive step at the age of 26 to leave Cameroon and travel to Europe. This decision was the result of both desperation and unyielding hope for a better future. He set out on a voyage that would permanently alter the course of his life with little more than ambition and resolve. He abandoned his comfortable surroundings in search of chances in France, where he believed he would be able to obtain the education and tools required to fulfill his aspirations.

The difficulties did not go away after moving to France; rather, they changed. As Ngannou moved to a new nation, he encountered a fresh set of challenges, including linguistic hurdles, cultural disparities, and the battle for survival. But no matter what, his hope for a brighter future continued to be his beacon. He threw himself into his training, giving mixed martial arts (MMA) his all attention. Recalling the dreams that had driven him on, he got closer to his objectives with every battle.

Ngannou's story is a living example of the strength of dreams and the indomitable spirit. In addition to changing his own life, his unwavering will to build a better future has inspired many others. He is living proof that a desire pursued with enthusiasm and tenacity can produce amazing results, despite all the challenges. As a champion today, he inspires others to follow their goals and overcome the limitations of their situation by embodying the optimism and possibility that dreams can come true.

Chapter 2: The Journey to Europe

A turning point in Francis Ngannou's life, the voyage to Europe symbolized both a leap of faith and a desperate attempt to realize his aspirations. Ngannou, at 26 years old, had to make the tough choice to leave Batié, Cameroon, behind in quest of brighter prospects, leaving behind friends and family. His decision was motivated by the knowledge that, even if he was passionate about boxing and mixed martial arts (MMA), staying would limit his potential due to the constraints of his surroundings.

We did not take Ngannou's departure lightly. He was both scared and filled with hope at the idea of leaving his own country. He was aware of the hazards associated with making such a journey, particularly in light of the unknowns that awaited. Still, his anxieties were surpassed by the promise of a better life, one in which he could follow his aspirations and provide for his family.

Lacking funds and supplies, Ngannou embarked on a difficult journey to reach Europe. There were obstacles on his path from the beginning. He encountered linguistic obstacles, cultural disparities, and the possibility of being exploited while traversing several nations. He faced emotional and physical challenges along the way, which put his resilience to the test.

Ngannou had to confront the difficult prospect of having to start over in a foreign country once he arrived in France. He felt alone and uncertain as he struggled to communicate and adjust to his new environment. But the will to succeed blazed brighter inside of him than any of the challenges he faced. He was prepared to go above and beyond in order to take advantage of this chance to realize his aspirations.

Ngannou got started in the MMA world by training at a nearby gym. He was driven to improve as a fighter despite the language barrier. His remarkable power and natural talent rapidly brought him attention. He soon started to establish himself in the neighborhood fighting scene by taking part in amateur matches and earning useful experience.

Traveling to Europe signified more than just a physical change for Ngannou; it also brought about a significant mental shift. His experiences along the road strengthened his conviction that perseverance and hard work are essential. Every obstacle he overcame helped him get closer to his ultimate objective of being a professional boxer.

Ngannou never forgot the sacrifices he had to make to attain this position as he advanced through the ranks. His trip was motivated by more than just self-interest; it was also a way to respect the aspirations of the people he left behind in Cameroon. In the future, he hoped to use his position to inspire others going through similar struggles and give back to the community.

In the end, Francis Ngannou's trip to Europe turned into a turning point in his life that prepared him to be a top athlete. His experiences molded his personality and gave him the fortitude required to succeed in the cutthroat world of mixed martial arts. His desire to improve the future for himself and the people he cared about drove him to use the lessons he had learned along the road as his profession developed.

Escaping Cameroon

Francis Ngannou did not decide to leave Cameroon lightly; it was the result of years spent battling destitution and little prospects. In his hometown of Batié, Ngannou's aspirations to become a professional fighter seemed more and more distant as he neared his mid-20s. He was on the verge of despair due to his family's ongoing hardships and the limitations of his surroundings. He understood that he had to escape the limitations of his situation to follow his dreams and build a better life.

Extreme bravery and tenacity were needed to flee Cameroon. Ngannou was aware that leaving his village would mean breaking off relationships with his friends, family, and culture. He was forced to take the chance by the possibility of a better future, overriding his fear of the unknown. He chose to go off on a voyage that would alter the course of his life, bearing a heavy heart but also an optimistic spirit.

Ngannou prepared his escape by carefully mapping out his path to Europe. He relied on accounts from people who had traveled a similar distance in order to find out information about possible routes. He had little money, so he saved what he could and embarked on his journey, knowing full well that it would be difficult and unpredictable.

The trip was dangerous. Ngannou traversed many nations, acclimating to strange landscapes and customs. He faced several challenges on the journey, such as language hurdles and the possibility of being taken advantage of. His perseverance was put to the test at every turn along the way, yet he never wavered in his dedication to his goals. His drive to succeed was strengthened by the challenges he encountered.

Ngannou thought about the sacrifices he was making while he was traveling. He understood that his achievement would not only transform his life but also have an effect on those he left behind, so he carried the weight of his family's aspirations and goals with him. He was driven forward even when the path seemed difficult by his strong desire to build a brighter future for himself and his loved ones.

Ngannou encountered the unpleasant reality of having to start over in a different country when he arrived in France. The thrill of his initial escape was soon overshadowed by the difficulties of survival and adaptation. He found daily living challenging due to the language barrier and cultural differences. Nevertheless, he found comfort in the realm of combat sports despite these hardships.

Ngannou started out training at a nearby gym, where he soon became well-known for his remarkable strength and knockout ability. His career started as a professional when his innate talent was recognized and he started fighting in amateur matches. What had started out as a means of getting out of poverty was becoming a route to prosperity?

Ngannou's experience of leaving Cameroon was more than simply a travel; it was a life-changing event that altered her identity. He developed a strong sense of perseverance and purpose as a result of the struggles he faced along the road. He acquired a determination to overcome life's obstacles that would help him in the cutthroat world of mixed martial arts.

In the end, Ngannou's flight from Cameroon proved to be a turning point in his life. His breakthrough as a UFC champion was made possible by a leap of faith that allowed him to realize his full potential. He kept the lessons he had learned from his voyage with him as he advanced through the ranks, always driven by the desire to encourage others to overcome obstacles and follow their passions.

Harsh Realities of Migrant Life

Following his escape from Cameroon and his arrival in France, Francis Ngannou encountered the hard reality of life as a migrant. The idea of being a professional boxer was thrilling, but adjusting to life in a foreign nation presented enormous obstacles. Ngannou soon discovered that achieving his goals would require overcoming several obstacles that would put his fortitude and tenacity to the test.

Ngannou had many of the same challenges as other migrants when he first arrived. The language barrier was one of the biggest obstacles. His lack of fluency in the language made it challenging for him to interact with others, carry out everyday duties, and communicate effectively. His sense of helplessness and annoyance increased due to his seclusion as he attempted to acclimatize to a strange place.

Ngannou additionally experienced financial difficulties. He had to figure out how to make ends meet as a newcomer in a place where living expenses were high. To make money, he took on odd jobs and frequently put in long hours in physically taxing positions. Despite being essential, these jobs took up a lot of his time and energy, which prevented him from concentrating on his training and fighting enthusiasm.

Another level of complexity was added by the combat scene's competitive nature. Ngannou soon discovered that it was difficult to make a name for himself in the French mixed martial arts scene. He had to put his limits to the test against seasoned boxers and demanding training schedules. Even though he had inherent talent, he felt pressure to uphold his reputation against more experienced opponents. Every fight offered a chance, but there was also anticipation pressure.

Ngannou also struggled with cultural displacement and homesickness. He missed his family, friends, and familiar surroundings and missed the comforts of home. At times of uncertainty, he was plagued by flashbacks to his happy and difficult boyhood in Cameroon. But instead of giving in to hopelessness, he channeled these emotions into motivation to work even harder through practice and competition.

Ngannou found strength in his prior experiences throughout this difficult time. His experiences in Cameroon had given him a strong sense of perseverance and a steadfast faith in the prospect of a brighter future. He used the emotional and physical obstacles as opportunities for personal development, channeling his troubles into his training. Every obstacle he faced served as a springboard to advance him on his quest.

Through overcoming the difficult circumstances of his migration, Ngannou made friends with other fighters and coaches who appreciated his skill and commitment. He felt a sense of belonging and support from these interactions, which helped him create a network that would help him grow in his job. His ability to persevere in the face of difficulty started to pay off when he started to establish himself in the local combat scene.

Ngannou's migration experiences influenced his outlook on achievement and life. He gained an appreciation for the worth of tenacity, hard effort, and the potential of dreams. With every obstacle he overcame, his will to accomplish his objectives and motivate those in such circumstances was strengthened. The journey represented hope for individuals who dared to dream beyond their circumstances, rather than only being about achieving personal accomplishment.

In the end, Ngannou's experience as a migrant was a crucible that helped shape him into the champion he would become. Through his experiences, he learned that although there are obstacles in the way of achievement, one has the inner strength to overcome them. As a well-known fighter of today, he represents the tenacity and resolve of many migrants who have the audacity to follow their aspirations in spite of all obstacles.

Homelessness and Perseverance in Paris

Francis Ngannou was homeless when he first arrived in Paris, a hard and frequently brutal reality that would eventually mold his character and resolve. Being a migrant without a permanent location to call home, he was forced to navigate life in a dangerous circumstance with few resources and no established support network. This difficult time put his fortitude and dedication to his goals to the test.

Ngannou experienced insecurity and uncertainty during his early days in Paris. All he had when he arrived was hope and determination, but circumstances soon caught up with him. He had no choice but to sleep in parks and on benches because he lacked the money to rent a house. Becoming homeless was an emotionally and physically trying experience for me. His mental health suffered as a result of his ongoing battle for security and safety, but he refused to allow hopelessness to define who he was.

Ngannou showed amazing tenacity in the face of these obstacles. He realized that achieving his goal of being a professional boxer would take sacrifice and unflinching dedication. He overcame the discomforts of his living situation every day and awoke with a fresh feeling of purpose. He looked for training facilities and became fully absorbed in the mixed martial arts community, using his training program as a way to vent his emotions and struggles.

Ngannou frequently depended on the goodwill of onlookers and other combatants to survive. He found support and a sense of belonging in the fighting community's brotherhood during a turbulent period. The concept that community and resiliency may help overcome adversity was reinforced when several gym patrons gave him shared meals or temporary refuge. These relationships not only helped him make friends but also inspired him to stick to his objectives.

For Ngannou, training turned into a means of escape and a means of turning his hardships into something constructive. He put in a tonne of effort in the gym, frequently working long hours to improve his abilities and push his physical boundaries. Every drop of perspiration symbolized his will to overcome his situation. His resolve was reinforced and he was better able to deal with the realities of homelessness because of the discipline and attention he developed throughout these demanding training sessions.

Despite the enormous challenges he encountered, Ngannou never lost sight of his goals. He took part in neighborhood bouts, each one giving him a glimmer of optimism and the possibility of a better future. His confidence and recognition increased with each victory, and he eventually carved out a place for himself in the world of competitive fighting. His ambition to achieve was bolstered by the difficulties of homelessness, which served as a constant reminder of the life he wished to create.

Ngannou's persistence eventually started to pay off. Opportunities began to arise as his fighting prowess garnered recognition. Better training facilities were obtained by him, and he started generating a steady income from fights and sponsorships. The immigrant who had been destitute was becoming a promising boxer as a result of the lessons he had learned from his experiences.

Through his time spent homeless in Paris, Ngannou gained priceless insight into the value of community, empathy, and resilience. It strengthened his conviction that persistence might result in achievement, regardless of how hopeless the situation appeared. As a champion today, Ngannou personifies the spirit of people who overcome hardship and shows that greatness can be attained by rising from the abyss of despair with perseverance and hard effort. Many people find inspiration in his narrative, which serves as a reminder that hope can shine through even the darkest circumstances.

Chapter 3: Discovering MMA

Francis Ngannou's life underwent a sea change when he was introduced to mixed martial arts (MMA). He began to focus on chasing a seemingly unachievable ideal instead of dwelling on his previous struggles. After landing in Paris and overcoming the challenges of homelessness, Ngannou was looking for a method to turn his love of fighting into a successful career when he happened upon MMA. This would prove to be a pivotal finding that would set him on the route to success.

Ngannou first learned about mixed martial arts (MMA) at a neighborhood gym, when he ran into some fighters who saw potential in his innate athleticism. He made the decision to give it a shot after being drawn in by the training environment's intensity. What started as a straightforward investigation into a new sport soon sparked a strong love in him. He found solace in MMA's punching, grappling, and all-around intensity, which gave him a way to express his frustrations and aspirations.

Ngannou saw right away as he started MMA training that the sport would allow him to combine his passion for fighting with a disciplined competitive environment. He was fascinated by the technical components of mixed martial arts (MMA) and devoted his life to learning boxing, kickboxing, wrestling, and Brazilian jiu-jitsu. He applied the same unwavering resolve that had defined his path thus far to every training session, drawing inspiration from his past setbacks to push himself to new limits.

Ngannou showed early in his training that he had a natural flair for striking. He stands out for his explosive power and athleticism, which help him perform well in sparring and contests. His promise was recognized by coaches and other fighters, who encouraged him to continue with the sport. The sense of having his skills acknowledged marked a significant change from the uncertainty and struggles he had experienced as a homeless immigrant. It gave him direction and a feeling of purpose, which fuelled his drive for success.

Ngannou gained insight into self-control, perseverance, and the value of having a strong work ethic while immersing himself in the world of mixed martial arts. The demanding training program required mental toughness in addition to physical strength. He was surrounded by fighters and instructors who were encouraging and had a crucial role in his growth. He felt like he belonged because of this camaraderie, which inspired him to work even harder in his training and pursue greatness.

Ngannou's big break came when he started taking part in amateur mixed martial arts matches. Every game gave him a chance to show off his abilities and gain more experience in the cage. He soon gained recognition for his strong hitting and perseverance, and MMA organizations and promoters started to take an interest in him. His confidence increased with every win, and the goal of turning a pro fighter into a reality got closer.

Not only did Ngannou's life change after learning about MMA, but it also changed who he was. From being a destitute immigrant, he turned into a focused athlete who wanted to win a global championship. He had a platform to transform his struggles and experiences into something worthwhile thanks to the sport. It enabled him to rewrite his story and transform hardship into strength.

Ngannou eventually found success in MMA, which acted as a trigger for his transformation from believing success was unattainable to attainable. His story is proof of the transformational power of sport and the strength of tenacity. As a well-known UFC champion today, Ngannou is a living example of the idea that success can be attained in the face of hardship by perseverance, hard effort, devotion, and a passion for one's goals.

Introduction to Martial Arts

An important element of Francis Ngannou's path was his introduction to martial arts before he rose to become one of the most feared fighters in mixed martial arts. Ngannou was always drawn to physical difficulties as a child growing up in Cameroon, but his early infatuation with boxing ignited his love for combat sports. He looked up to renowned fighters like Mike Tyson, whose strength, power, and dedication struck a deep chord with him, as did many other young boys in his village. The basis for his ultimate discovery of martial arts was laid by this desire.

Ngannou was first introduced to martial arts in an informal setting. Even though there were few official training facilities available to him in Cameroon, he managed to release some of his energy by organizing impromptu boxing matches with acquaintances. Despite being unstructured, these early encounters gave him a competitive attitude and showed him his untapped fighting ability. Ngannou's passion for combat sports grew despite the lack of appropriate gear and training, and he started to envision a time when he might take up fighting more seriously.

But Ngannou's journey towards a career in professional martial arts didn't start to take shape until he got to France. He made it to a Parisian gym following a trying time of homelessness and hardship. He first experienced martial arts in their purest form here. He discovered mixed martial arts (MMA) at the gym, a sport that fused his love of boxing as a youth with new skills like kickboxing, jiu-jitsu, and wrestling.

Ngannou had a strong connection to the sport the moment he walked inside the gym. He found an organized setting in mixed martial arts (MMA) to polish his innate ability. His exposure to martial arts taught him discipline, attention, and resilience in addition to how to fight. He was captivated by the blend of several combat methods and accepted the challenge of being an expert in every facet of the sport.

Ngannou's remarkable potential was evident from his early training sessions. His natural strength, athleticism, and eagerness to pick things up impressed the coaches. His striking prowess soon made him a formidable weapon in boxing, but he was equally focused on honing his grappling and submission skills. Martial arts became more for Ngannou than a method to survive; they allowed him to change his life and follow the aspirations he had carried since he was a young boy.

He was able to advance as a martial artist because of the disciplined instruction and guidance he got in Paris. His determination to make up for lost time and establish his worth drove him to immerse himself in every facet of the sport. Martial arts developed into a career and a philosophy of tenacity, imparting to Ngannou the values of perseverance, hard effort, and maintaining one's modesty in the face of achievement.

Martial arts provided Ngannou with a fresh start. It provided him with a feeling of direction and a network of like-minded fighters. He was a young man with a desire to become a disciplined athlete on the route to becoming a champion, and this introduction to martial arts was the key that opened the door to his destiny. Ngannou's experience in martial arts is evidence of his tenacity and willpower. He is a top-tier fighter now, but his achievement stems from those formative years when he overcame obstacles in his background and set out on a new path to greatness thanks to the unadulterated power of martial arts.

First Steps in the MMA World

With his foray into the realm of mixed martial arts (MMA), Francis Ngannou embarked on a journey characterized by tenacity, self-control, and swift development. Following his battles with homelessness in Paris, Ngannou was able to not only survive but also flourish when he came across mixed martial arts. Although his initial forays into the sport were fraught with difficulties, they also set the groundwork for his eventual ascent to become one of the world's most formidable fighters.

The Parisian gym where Ngannou took sanctuary and started training was the source of his first exposure to mixed martial arts. His primary concentration at first was boxing, a sport he had long loved while growing up in Cameroon. But he was drawn to the mixed martial arts (MMA) scene because of its use of grappling, hitting, and submission tactics. Despite lacking official training in martial arts disciplines such as Brazilian jiu-jitsu or wrestling, Ngannou entered mixed martial arts (MMA) with the same intense drive that had gotten him through his previous struggles.

Ngannou had little prior experience, yet his inherent skills were apparent right away. He stood out in sparring sessions thanks to his explosive power and athleticism, and his trainers saw potential in him right away. Despite being somewhat new to the sport, Ngannou made quick improvements because of his desire to pick things up and adjust. His daily visits to the gym turned into opportunities for personal development as he became fully absorbed in the striking, ground fighting, and submission techniques of mixed martial arts.

Ngannou stood out from other would-be boxers because of his work ethic. He was motivated to seize every opportunity because he had faced so much hardship in his life. He devoted endless hours to perfecting his technique, learning everything he could from his teammates and teachers. He trained hard at the beginning of the sport, pushing himself to the limit both emotionally and physically.

Ngannou had to learn how to handle the mental demands of the sport in addition to the technical skills of mixed martial arts. Fighters in mixed martial arts must possess a strong mental toughness since they have to maintain composure under duress and change tactics fast. Because of his difficult prior experiences, Ngannou already had a solid metal foundation. He took the same fortitude into the cage because he knew how to endure hardship.

During his early MMA career, Ngannou's first amateur battles were crucial matches. He gained priceless experience from each fight, which enabled him to better comprehend the difficulties of fighting in a cage and apply what he had learned to actual combat scenarios. He soon gained notoriety as a knockout artist thanks to his potent attacks, and professional MMA organizations soon began to take notice.

Ngannou developed his technique as he competed and got bigger, fusing better grappling techniques with his deadly knockout power. His early cage successes demonstrated his capacity to change and grow as he put in many hours to complete his skill set and become a more formidable fighter. His early successes helped him advance and gave him the self-assurance to turn a professional MMA fighter into a full-time job.

Ngannou made quick growth and showed steadfast dedication to his dream during his early MMA steps. He was resolved to make the most of his second chance at life, which the sport had granted him. Those who trained with him saw that he had the potential to be something special, even though he was still relatively fresh to the world of professional fighting.

The foundation for Ngannou's ultimate ascent to the top of MMA was built throughout these early years. His commitment, together with his innate skill and unwavering work ethic, made him a warrior to watch. Throughout his career, the early lessons he learned about discipline, attention, and overcoming hardship would guide him toward the greatness he was destined to attain.

Early Training and Challenges

Early on in his mixed martial arts (MMA) training, Francis Ngannou faced many challenges in addition to extreme dedication. He knew he was beginning from scratch the moment he walked into the Paris gym because he had no formal training in martial arts like Brazilian jiu-jitsu, wrestling, or Muay Thai. Ngannou faced a high learning curve in the sport, but his innate athleticism and unwavering will to succeed helped him to advance swiftly.

Ngannou's initial big obstacle was getting used to the MMA's technical requirements. He was a strong striker due to his sheer strength, but he lacked grappling and ground fighting skills. Because of this, he was exposed to circumstances where strategy and technique were just as crucial as brute force. Ngannou, however, met these obstacles head-on with the same tenacity that had seen him through his share of adversity. He worked with his teachers for extended periods, honing his skills in takedown defense, submissions, and technique. For Ngannou, training in Paris also meant financial challenges. He was an underprivileged immigrant who had come and could not afford the costly training materials or fees. Thankfully, many of his gym friends and trainers acknowledged his ability and promise and offered to help. Some gave Ngannou free training sessions, while others gave him equipment so he could concentrate only on improving as a fighter.

Even with the assistance, Ngannou had a demanding early training schedule in terms of both mental and physical strain. His body could no longer withstand the rigorous training needed for mixed martial arts. His incessant training regimen and the requirement to become proficient in several disciplines put his resilience to the test. Ngannou also had to deal with the emotional strain of combat. He had to train his mind as well as his body for the sport, learning how to maintain composure under duress and concentrate during battles.

Ngannou had difficulties not just in his training but also in his journey because of his unknown future. Not having much money, there was a lot of pressure to be successful in mixed martial arts. He endured the physical and mental strain of training because he was afraid that failure would mean going back to a life of poverty. He battled every day in the gym to realize his dream and to have the opportunity to move on from his past struggles.

Ngannou's early career underwent significant changes, one of which was his realization that MMA required strategy and adaptation in addition to pure force. He started to pay more attention to the sport, attending bouts and picking the brains of more seasoned competitors. He advanced quickly because of his capacity to take in new skills and modify them to fit his natural fighting style. His teachers were astounded at how fast he was able to incorporate intricate moves into his training, such as offensive combos and defensive grappling methods.

Ngannou's early challenges paid off as he started fighting in amateur competitions. He was a formidable opponent because of his strength and tenacity, and his technical development gave him the ability to outclass opponents on the ground as well as standing. With every battle, he gained fresh insights and experiences that improved his powers and bolstered his self-assurance.

Through these early setbacks, Ngannou was able to cultivate the toughness and determination that would serve as the foundation for his professional fighting career. He knew that being successful in mixed martial arts (MMA) needed more than simply physical strength; it also required self-control, selflessness, and an unwavering faith in oneself. Ngannou never wavered from his objective of becoming a champion, even in the face of obstacles during his training.

These early years set the groundwork for Ngannou's future as a fighter. He became a more complete and formidable athlete as a result of overcoming the challenges he faced in his early training, which equipped him for the fights he would face on his path to becoming the greatest mixed martial artist in history.

Chapter 4: Rise in the UFC

The Ultimate Fighting Championship (UFC) saw a phenomenal surge in Francis Ngannou's career. Ngannou's ascent to worldwide fame began with his UFC debut, having spent years perfecting his craft and conquering great personal obstacles. His unwavering work ethic, physical strength, and dedication to learning every facet of mixed martial arts (MMA) were the defining characteristics of his ascent to the top.

After making his UFC debut in December 2015, Ngannou quickly gained the interest of the mixed martial arts community. Ngannou showed off his incredible knockout power in his first bout against Luis Henrique, finishing him with a powerful uppercut in the second round. This triumph offered a preview of an athlete who could rule the heavyweight class in the future.

Ngannou was unique among fighters not only because of his knockout power but also because of how quickly he advanced in the sport. Even though Ngannou's experience in mixed martial arts was limited, he was able to swiftly adjust to the intricacies of the UFC's heavyweight class. He was a problem for opponents because of his natural striking ability and raw agility. His early bouts frequently resulted in vicious knockouts, which led to his being dubbed "The Predator."

Ngannou's successes became more remarkable as he rose through the ranks. He squared off against one of the heavyweight division's best young talents, Curtis Blaydes, in 2016. After Blaydes was unable to continue due to eye injuries, Ngannou controlled the fight and won by TKO. Ngannou's standing as a viable competitor in the category was strengthened by this victory.

When Ngannou squared up against former Strikeforce and K-1 World Grand Prix champion Alistair Overeem in 2017, it was one of the most pivotal moments of his UFC career. Before the bout, many considered Overeem to be among the heavyweight division's most lethal strikers, but Ngannou shocked the mixed martial arts community with one of the most brutal knockouts in UFC history. Ngannou's single uppercut knocked Overeem to the canvas, instantly catapulting Ngannou into the picture's title. The knockout cemented Ngannou's status as the strongest puncher in the sport and earned him the title of "Knockout of the Year" from numerous sites.

Due to his outstanding results, Ngannou faced then-champion Stipe Miocic for a chance to win the UFC heavyweight title early in 2018. But Ngannou had a reality check from the battle. Miocic had an amazing run of knockouts, but his skill and experience as a wrestler proved to be too much. By using his grappling to control the battle, Miocic was able to neutralize Ngannou's strength and win by unanimous decision. Ngannou was humbled by the defeat and realized that he still needed to work on certain aspects of his game.

Ngannou returned to the drawing board, determined to make a stronger impression this time. He put in a tonne of effort to raise his fight IQ overall, cardio, and wrestling skills. He learned a lot about patience, strategy, and the value of being a well-rounded fighter from his defeat to Miocic. The extent of Ngannou's learning would be shown in his subsequent encounters.

Ngannou went on another great run in the years that followed, easily defeating strong opponents. The majority of the battles ended in the first round, with fighters like Cain Velasquez, Junior dos Santos, and Jairzinho Rozenstruik succumbing to Ngannou's devastating power. He was one of the most feared fighters in UFC history because of his capability to dispatch opponents swiftly and viciously.

Ngannou's career completed a full circle in 2021 when he fought Miocic again at UFC 260 for the heavyweight championship. Ngannou was a different warrior this time. By enhanced wrestling defense, enhanced conditioning, and a more methodical approach, Ngannou outclassed Miocic and successfully eliminated him in the second round to claim the title of UFC heavyweight champion. Ngannou's journey from the streets of Cameroon to the biggest stage in the world was realized with the victory, which marked the apex of his UFC career.

The development of Ngannou in the UFC is a tale of progress, tenacity, and the unwavering quest for excellence. Ngannou's journey—from his lowly beginnings to his time as the heavyweight champion—is proof of the strength of perseverance and hard effort. He is still regarded as one of the world's most feared and revered boxers today, and millions of people are still motivated by his legacy.

Debut Fights

From a raw, strong fighter to one of the most feared knockout artists in mixed martial arts (MMA), Francis Ngannou's UFC debuts signaled the start of his remarkable journey. Following his triumph over major personal setbacks and his training in Paris, Ngannou joined the UFC with a reputation for having devastating striking power and a burning desire to prove himself on the largest stage in the world.

On December 19, 2015, at UFC on Fox 17, Ngannou made his UFC debut against grappling expert Luis Henrique, a Brazilian fighter. For a novice like Ngannou, especially given his lack of prior MMA experience, it was a difficult matchup. Nonetheless, Ngannou demonstrated why he was a fighter to watch right away in the first exchanges of the bout. Henrique tried to use wrestling and clinch work to control the fight, but Ngannou stayed composed and patient, keeping Henrique at bay with his hitting. Ngannou found his window in the second round and floored Henrique with a hard uppercut. Ngannou's decisive win immediately made him famous and announced the advent of a possible heavyweight contender.

After winning his first bout, Ngannou faced another promising heavyweight prospect, Curtis Blaydes, at UFC bout Night 86 on April 10, 2016. Blaydes presented Ngannou with an alternative kind of challenge because of his reputation for wrestling and grappling. But Ngannou was able to control the battle with his punches once more. Blaydes was hit hard by him during the first two rounds, causing his eye to swell shut and the doctor to break up the bout. Ngannou was given the TKO victory, solidifying his status as a formidable opponent in the category.

Ngannou's subsequent fight took place at UFC on Fox 20 on July 23, 2016, against Bojan Mihajlović. It was another challenge for Ngannou, but his opponent was unable to withstand his powerful strikes. After little more than a minute of action in the opening round, Ngannou quickly dispatched Mihajlović by throwing a barrage of punches. The victory demonstrated his ability to stop fights early and continued his winning streak.

Ngannou, who was still on the rise, went up against Anthony Hamilton at UFC Fight Night 102 on December 9, 2016. This battle highlighted Ngannou's developing skill set. Rather than depending just on his strikes, Ngannou used a submission to take the first round, catching Hamilton with a kimura. It was an indication that Ngannou was becoming a more versatile fighter who could prevail in a variety of ways.

Highlight-reel knockouts and dominant performances marked Ngannou's early UFC battles, which swiftly established his reputation as one of the sport's most dangerous heavyweights. His early victories prepared the way for his ascent to the top of the category and made him a fighter that both observers and fighters wanted to watch.

These early bouts not only demonstrated Ngannou's unadulterated strength but also suggested that he would develop into a fully-fledged combatant. With every victory, he moved one step closer to his aim of becoming the heavyweight champion and gained momentum in his ascent to the top of the UFC rankings.

Gaining Recognition

Francis Ngannou became known as one of the most thrilling and dangerous competitors in the heavyweight class as he kept winning matches in the UFC. Because of his unmatched strength, agility, and knockout power, he became a fan favorite and a rising star in the mixed martial arts (MMA) world. Ngannou's tendency to end contests brutally—often in the opening few minutes of the fight—set him apart from many other heavyweights.

Ngannou's run of knockout wins started to generate talk within the UFC as well as among supporters. His impressive fighting technique drew notice, and his commanding performances elevated him to the status of a top prospect. Although he made waves in the heavyweight category with his early victories against Curtis Blaydes, Bojan Mihajlović, and Anthony Hamilton, it was his knockout of Andrei Arlovski in January 2017 that made his global debut.

When Ngannou faced Arlovski, the former heavyweight champion of the UFC, at UFC on Fox 23, he faced the more seasoned veteran without fear. Ngannou delivered a potent series of punches in less than a minute, sending Arlovski sprawling to the ground. The knockout put Ngannou on the radar as a legitimate contender for the heavyweight title and was another highlight-reel performance for him. His strength astounded spectators and pundits, and many started to predict that he would win in the future.

But Ngannou's success went beyond his knockouts. His inspiring tale of being a Cameroonian immigrant who overcame hardship and homelessness to succeed struck a chord with people all across the world. Ngannou gained respect throughout the sport for his modest outside-the-cage manner and his unwavering commitment to honing his talents within. With the rise in his fame came increased expectations for him.

When Ngannou squared off against one of the most accomplished heavyweight fighters in MMA history, Alistair Overeem, later in 2017, it was the real turning point in his career. Despite Overeem's reputation for skill and experience as a striker and former K-1 and Strikeforce champion, Ngannou pulled off one of the most vicious knockouts in UFC history. Ngannou stunned the MMA world by sending Overeem flying to the canvas with a single uppercut. He was awarded "Performance of the Night" for the knockout, which further cemented his status as the UFC's deadliest hitter.

Ngannou was now unquestionably recognized as one of the heavyweight title's leading contenders after his victory over Overeem. He had built a sizable fan base thanks to his knockout run, and they were excited to see him contend for the title. In addition, the UFC acknowledged Ngannou's star potential by showcasing him extensively in marketing materials and chronicling his amazing rise from poverty to the verge of world championship contention.

Ngannou's remarkable life story and his in-cage performances contributed to his ascent to fame. His fan base grew outside of the UFC's typical demographic as he became more well-known, and his knockout ability became legendary inside the sport. Ngannou was already regarded as one of the most dangerous fighters in the division when he earned his first championship chance in 2018, and many people thought it would only be a matter of time until he won UFC gold.

During this phase of his career, Ngannou became not only a world-class heavyweight boxer but also a global sporting icon. Together with his amazing fighting prowess, his ability to relate to fans made sure he would go down as one of the UFC's most fascinating and engaging characters.

The Knockout Artist

A string of stunning, highlight-reel finishes that stunned opponents and viewers alike solidified Francis Ngannou's status as the most dangerous knockout artist in mixed martial arts (MMA). Ngannou, known as "The Predator," gained notoriety for his unadulterated, explosive strength that appeared almost supernatural as he methodically defeated some of the hardest-hit heavyweight competitors.

Ngannou showed off his striking prowess as soon as he entered the UFC, but what set him apart was the power of his blows. His knockouts were more than just wins; they made a lasting impression. Few of his opponents were able to successfully elude his power, even if they were aware that they had to do so. Ngannou swiftly gained notoriety for his ability to finish fights with a single blow.

At UFC 218 in December 2017, he faced Alistair Overeem in one of his most memorable performances. For Ngannou, facing the seasoned striker Overeem—who has years of experience—was a big test. But in the opening frame, Ngannou landed one of the most vicious uppercuts in UFC history, knocking Overeem out in a brutal finish that was constantly reenacted. With the knockout, Ngannou gained international recognition and the title of UFC's top knockout artist, and the match instantly became a classic. Later on, it received the 2017 "Knockout of the Year" award.

Ngannou had a simple but incredibly potent style: he would wait for the right moment to land a blow, and when he did, it would frequently result in an immediate knockout.

His opponents were under tremendous pressure to land clean, powerful strikes early in the fight because they knew that even the slightest error may result in their elimination. Because of his opponents' inability to stand up to his strength, Ngannou's opponents lost a lot of his fights in the opening round.

One-punch finishes weren't the only way he knocked people out. Ngannou demonstrated his skill by dispatching opponents with uppercuts, hooks, and straight punches. His tremendous strikes knocked out fighters like Curtis Blaydes, Cain Velasquez, and Junior dos Santos within minutes of the bell ringing. Ngannou's status as the most feared fighter in the heavyweight class was further cemented by his effortless finishing of seasoned veterans and past champions.

Not only did his knockout streak provide remarkable outcomes, but it also demonstrated a remarkable finishing technique. Ngannou frequently delivered knockouts that were so vicious and decisive that they shocked both the spectators and his other competitors. It became evident that Ngannou was a force of nature, and that no heavyweight in the UFC was safe from him.

The fact that Ngannou maintained his composure under duress made him much more dangerous. Ngannou displayed patience by waiting for the ideal opportunity to attack, in contrast to many knockout artists who rely on reckless, forceful strikes. His unmatched strength and ability to time everything perfectly made him an intimidating presence in the cage.

During his career, Ngannou's ability to finish opponents via knockout earned him a spot among the UFC's elite, and his strength became the stuff of legends. Due to his remarkable ability to end fights, "The Predator" became a highly sought-after fighter. Fans went to see him compete because they expected to witness another incredible knockout. Ngannou was already regarded as one of the most dangerous knockout artists in combat sports history before he won the UFC heavyweight championship.

Ngannou's reputation as "The Knockout Artist" is still one of his most memorable achievements in the UFC; it's evidence of his unmatched strength and capacity to turn a fight around with a single blow. Whether it was with a stunning hook, a massive uppercut, or a clean right hand, Ngannou's knockouts are a testament to his greatness and will go down as some of the most amazing events in UFC history.

Chapter 5: Becoming UFC Heavyweight Champion

The story of Francis Ngannou's ascent to the UFC Heavyweight Championship is one of tenacity, resolve, and unwavering ambition. In preparation for his title attempt, Ngannou realized that his ultimate goal—becoming wealthy and homeless as well as mastering the difficulties of adjusting to a new sport—was within reach, having overcome major setbacks throughout his life.

The road to the title officially started when Ngannou captivated the UFC with his electric performances and knockout strength. Following a string of outstanding wins—among which included noteworthy TKOs of well-known opponents like Alistair Overeem and Junior dos Santos—Ngannou was granted a crack at the heavyweight championship in January 2018, when he faced then-champion

Stipe Miocic. In addition to trying to win the title, he also had the chance to exact revenge on Miocic, who had defeated him earlier in 2018.

Ngannou and Miocic squared up in a match that would put both fighters' skills and mental toughness to the test at UFC 220. Ngannou, who was known for being a knockout artist, found it difficult to match Miocic's fighting style and fighting intelligence and lost by unanimous decision. Ngannou was humbled by the loss, but he didn't let it ruin his career—rather, he seized the opportunity to get better. Realizing that he needed to be more than just a strong attacker, he committed himself to improving his wrestling techniques and fighting style.

Over the ensuing years, Ngannou showed notable advancements in his range of abilities. He kept winning by knockout, demonstrating his development as a fighter. Particularly noteworthy was Ngannou's victory over former champion Cain Velasquez at UFC on ESPN 1 in February 2019. Ngannou knocked out

Velasquez in just 26 seconds, solidifying his place among the top contenders. This performance prepared the audience for the much awaited rematch with Miocic, as did victories against Jairzinho Rozenstruik and Alexander Volkov later on.

At UFC 260 in March 2021, Ngannou and Miocic eventually had their highly anticipated rematch. The battle was important because it was for the heavyweight title, but it was also an opportunity for Ngannou to show that he had changed since their first meeting. Ngannou showed a newfound level of poise and strategy as the fight progressed. He waited patiently for his chance, making good use of his enhanced wrestling defense and striking technique.

Ngannou found his opening in round two. He landed a vicious series of blows, including a strong left hook that knocked Miocic to the ground. The knowledge that Ngannou was now the new UFC Heavyweight Champion dawned on everyone as the referee intervened to end the bout. Ngannou's life and career took a significant turn when he achieved this achievement, which was the result of years of sacrifice and hard effort.

Not only was Ngannou's victory as the UFC Heavyweight Champion a personal accomplishment, but it was also a historic one for the sport. As the first fighter of African descent to win the UFC heavyweight championship, Ngannou served as an inspiration and source of hope for a great number of people worldwide. His rise from a tiny Cameroonian town to the top of the MMA ranks is proof of the strength of tenacity and willpower.

Ngannou accepted his position as champion with humility, understanding that the title carried some responsibility. He frequently thought back on his experience and used his position to encourage those who were facing hardship. Fans saw great resonance in Ngannou's story, which went beyond the realm of mixed martial arts to touch on universal themes of adversity, tenacity, and victory.

He vowed to defend his championship against the strongest opponents in the heavyweight class during his stint as champion. Ngannou kept stressing the value of perseverance and hard effort while highlighting the traits that had propelled him to the top.

In conclusion, the story of Francis Ngannou's rise to the title of UFC Heavyweight Champion is a stirring one of triumphing over hardship and reaching greatness. His rise from modest beginnings to the top of the mixed martial arts world is an inspiration to both spectators and aspiring fighters, showing us all that anything is achievable with perseverance and drive.

The First Title Shot

Francis Ngannou met the current heavyweight champion Stipe Miocic at UFC 220 on January 20, 2018, for his first opportunity to win a title in the UFC. The explosive knockout power of Ngannou against the versatile skill set of Miocic—who excelled in wrestling, hitting, and experience—made this clash highly anticipated. Not only was it for the championship belt, but Ngannou also had the chance to establish himself on the biggest platform in mixed martial arts, making it a pivotal point in his career.

Ngannou was riding a wave of enthusiasm going into the battle, having won several noteworthy bouts. His exploits, which demonstrated his capacity to end fights with devastating knockouts, had drawn the interest of both fans and pundits. Ngannou was known as the strongest hitter in the sport going into the championship fight, and he was regarded as a formidable striker. He had to contend with the weight of pressure, too, as many people thought this was his chance to win the heavyweight championship.

Both competitors had some time to get to know one another before going up against Miocic. Ngannou was wary at first because he knew Miocic's advantages and the champion's prowess in the ring. But as the opening round went on, it was clear that Ngannou had changed from the aggressive, overpowering fighter he had been in the past. Miocic controlled the bout by using his wrestling and grappling skills to take Ngannou down several times and negate his striking potential.

Ngannou was a strong opponent when he entered the octagon, but he had trouble getting into a rhythm. As he persisted in pushing the action and controlling the fight's tempo, Miocic's strategy and expertise were evident. Ngannou was unable to take advantage of his strength, and his striking was less potent than it had been in earlier fights. After five rounds of action, Ngannou was declared the winner by unanimous decision, which was a major blow to his hopes of winning the heavyweight title.

This loss marked a turning point in Ngannou's life. It made him reassess his fighting style and skill set since he realized that to compete at the top level, he needed to improve his all-around game. Ngannou took the setback as an opportunity to grow rather than allow it to define him. He committed himself to being a more dangerous and versatile fighter by working to improve his cardio, fight IQ, and wrestling skills.

Undoubtedly disheartening, Ngannou's career took a drastic turn after the defeat to Miocic. Applying the principles he had learned from the battle to his training, he concentrated on becoming a fully-fledged mixed martial artist. This commitment to bettering himself set the stage for his eventual return to the top of the heavyweight class.

Ngannou learned a lot about the sport and himself from his first title run. Even though it was a difficult defeat, it eventually strengthened his will to make a better comeback. Regrouping and honing his craft, Ngannou proceeded to establish himself as one of the heavyweight division's elite contenders, finally earning another chance at the title and the chance to demonstrate his continued development as a fighter. His first title fight experience turned into a pivotal moment in his career, paving the way for his ultimate rise to the position of UFC Heavyweight Champion.

The Road to the Championship

Francis Ngannou's ascent to the UFC Heavyweight Championship is proof of his tenacity, diligence, and unyielding will. After suffering a humiliating loss in his first championship defense against Stipe Miocic at UFC 220, Ngannou embarked on a journey of self-improvement and concentrated preparation to restore his standing among the heavyweight division's top. The journey to the title required more than just physical preparation; it also required mental toughness and a dedication to growing from prior failures. Following his January 2018 defeat by Miocic, Ngannou had to make a significant career pivot. He was aware that expanding his skill set and developing as a fighter were essential to becoming a champion. Ngannou went back to the drawing board and committed to raising his fight intelligence in general, grappling, and wrestling. He received his training from renowned teachers at the Xtreme Couture MMA gym in Las Vegas, where he also sparred with top competitors. This was a training setting that gave Ngannou the tools and direction he needed to improve.

Ngannou's diligence started to show results. He fought Curtis Blaydes at UFC Fight Night 141 in November 2018 in his next bout. Ngannou confirmed his status as a top contender by demonstrating his improved talents with an impressive knockout just 45 seconds into the first round. The win made a big statement, showing that he was prepared to face the best in the division and had learned from his prior defeat.

Ngannou maintained his winning streak after defeating Blaydes by turning in a dominant performance against Cain Velasquez at the UFC on ESPN 1 in February 2019. Ngannou used a strong right hand to knock out the former heavyweight champion in a contest that lasted only 26 seconds. With this victory, Ngannou proved once again that he was a serious title contender and made it very evident to the heavyweight division that he was back and hungry.

The following fight was Ngannou vs. Rozenstruik at UFC 249 in May 2020. Rozenstruik was an unbeaten fighter with a reputation for his striking, so this bout was another crucial test for Ngannou. Ngannou defeated Rozenstruik in only twenty seconds, securing a commanding victory. The MMA community was riveted by the finish's quickness and intensity, which moved Ngannou one step closer to a rematch with the heavyweight championship.

Ngannou was once more in the title discussion as his knockout run gained traction. In light of his outstanding results, the UFC gave him a second chance to defend the heavyweight title against Stipe Miocic at UFC 260 in March 2021. There was a lot of excitement leading up to this battle because Ngannou might win back the championship and exact revenge on Miocic for his previous defeat.

Ngannou showed a profound awareness of his own strengths and renewed confidence in the run-up to the battle. From being a one-dimensional knockout artist, he had developed into a versatile fighter who could change his strategy. Ngannou felt ready to demonstrate the abilities he had honed over his training as fight night drew near.

At UFC 260, Ngannou made history when he entered the octagon. From his first championship chance, he had learned a lot and this time he was going to make the most of it. Ngannou showed off his growth as a boxer in the second round of the bout as he connected with a strong left hook that instantly knocked down Miocic. Ngannou knew his goal had come true as the referee intervened to end the bout and declare him the new UFC Heavyweight Champion.

Ngannou had many obstacles and disappointments on his path to the title, but in the end, his perseverance and commitment brought him to the top of the sport. Not only is his path from a small Cameroonian town to the UFC Heavyweight Championship an inspiring tale of perseverance, self-belief, and overcoming hardship, but it is also a story of athletic success. As a champion, Ngannou not only fulfilled his goals but also became an inspiration to others going through difficult times, demonstrating that anything is achievable with perseverance and hard effort.

Victory and Becoming the Heavyweight King

Francis Ngannou's long-time ambition came true on March 27, 2021, when he entered the octagon for a rematch against the current champion, Stipe Miocic, at UFC 260. The pressure was on for both Ngannou, who wanted to win the heavyweight championship, and Miocic, who wanted to establish himself as one of the best heavyweights in UFC history. Fans and observers were excited to witness how Ngannou's development as a fighter would play out at this crucial juncture as the fight drew near.

Both combatants warily exchanged blows as the battle got underway, with Ngannou looking calm and calculated. Ngannou demonstrated a more adaptable game plan than in their first meeting, utilizing feints and better footwork to generate gaps. Miocic tried to go for his typical wrestling-heavy style, but Ngannou's sharper senses and grappling experience kept the fight at the stand, where he was most at ease.

Ngannou kept his composure as the opening round went on, scoring big blows that seemed to tip the scales in his favor. He displayed not just his knockout strength but also an improved sense of Miocic's maneuvers. Ngannou started to show the confidence that his training and prior successes had given him.

The contest took a significant swing in the second round. Ngannou discovered the chance he had been waiting for, and his calmness and patience paid off. He connected cleanly with Miocic with a well-timed left hook, sending the champion flying to the canvas. As Ngannou continued to ground and pound after the huge hit, the referee intervened to end the bout and crowned Ngannou the new UFC Heavyweight Champion.

For Ngannou, it was an unbelievable occasion. Raising the championship belt above his head as he stood in the octagon, he symbolized his victory and arduous journey. The triumph signified the end of years of tenacity, selflessness, and unshakeable faith in oneself. Fans throughout the world were enthralled with Ngannou's journey from a small Cameroonian hamlet, through homelessness and hardships in Europe, to becoming the heavyweight king.

Ngannou paused after his triumph to consider his path. He thanked everyone who had helped him throughout the years, including his coaches, family, and supporters, after he won. He also thanked mixed martial arts for providing him with a platform to realize his aspirations. Because of his humility and appreciation for his heritage, Ngannou won over fans and became known as an inspiration as well as a champion.

After defeating Miocic, Ngannou made history by becoming the first fighter of African descent to hold the UFC Heavyweight Championship. This accomplishment had an impact well beyond the cage, serving as inspiration and hope for young fighters and those going through hardship anywhere in the world. Ngannou's tale became a symbol of hope, showing that anyone can overcome even the most difficult situations with perseverance, hard effort, and commitment.

Ngannou's reign as the heavyweight king was greeted with excitement about his upcoming title defenses. A high-stakes fight between the former heavyweight champion Jon Jones and other elite contenders was among the many matchups that fans excitedly anticipated. With his remarkable knockout power and developing skill set, Ngannou was a formidable champion, and the mixed martial arts community was eager to see how he would handle the difficulties that were ahead.

To sum up, Francis Ngannou's triumph at UFC 260 and his elevation to the Heavyweight Championship were the apex of an incredible journey characterized by tenacity, diligence, and unflinching faith. Ngannou realized his dream when he put on the championship belt, and he also inspired many others all over the world by demonstrating that greatness can be attained with hard work and determination.

Chapter 6: Fighting Style and Training

Francis Ngannou's fighting style is distinguished by his powerful knockout power, explosive hitting ability, and unwavering will to win. Ngannou, sometimes nicknamed "The Predator," is one of the most feared heavyweights in mixed martial arts (MMA) because of his fierceness in the octagon and his ability to end bouts swiftly. His style of fighting combines kickboxing and Muay Thai aspects with classic boxing methods, giving him the ability to deliver deadly blows from a variety of angles.

Power Strike

The most remarkable quality of Ngannou is his knockout power, which comes from his innate strength, explosive speed, and quickness. He has a long history of first-round knockout victories, frequently taking out opponents with a single blow. His remarkable hand speed complements his striking skills, enabling him to deliver potent strikes with unexpected rapidity. Ngannou's standout finishes over opponents such as Alistair Overeem and Stipe Miocic spoke to the deadly nature of his left hook and right cross.

Steps and Motion

Ngannou's striking is his main strength, but he has also significantly improved his movement and footwork. He frequently moved forward aggressively early in his career, relying primarily on his power. But after losing to Miocic in his first championship defense, Ngannou realized he had to improve as a fighter all around. He started enhancing his striking technique with lateral movement, feints, and distance control, which made it harder for opponents to confront him.

Grabbing and Wrestling

Ngannou has spent a lot of work honing his wrestling and grappling techniques, even if striking is his main focus. Recognizing that top heavyweights would try to take the fight to the canvas, he put a lot of effort into improving his defensive wrestling skills. He gained valuable takedown defense skills from training with seasoned grapplers and wrestlers, which helped him maintain the fight standing, where he shines. He can now switch positions and get out of hazardous situations thanks to his enhanced grappling abilities, which makes him a more adaptable combatant.

Exercise Plans

Ngannou's rigorous and thorough training schedule demonstrates his dedication to being the greatest. He divides his time between strength and conditioning, grappling, wrestling, and striking. Typical training sessions consist of:

Striking Drills: Ngannou spends a lot of time honing combinations, pads, and heavy bag work. He is primarily concerned with improving technique, speed, and power. He often practices under the guidance of knowledgeable teachers and sparring partners to mimic combat situations.

Specializing in takedown defense, escapes, and grappling skills, Ngannou devotes a portion of his training to these activities. This makes him more versatile and ready to face opponents who could try to take advantage of holes in his ground game.

Conditioning: To improve his physical capabilities, Ngannou combines a variety of strength and conditioning routines. To increase endurance, explosiveness, and general fitness, this involves weightlifting, high-intensity interval training (HIIT), and aerobic exercises.

Mental Conditioning: Ngannou is aware of the significance of mental training in combat sports. He frequently uses mental exercises and visualization techniques to get ready for the psychological demands of competition.

Recuperation: An essential component of Ngannou's training regimen is recovery. To make sure his body can withstand the demanding demands of training and competition, he places a high priority on rest and recovery. This covers stretching, massage therapy, and a healthy diet.

Combat Intelligence

Along with his physical characteristics, Ngannou's fighting intelligence has improved dramatically throughout his career. He is now more adept at reading opponents, planning moves ahead of time, and making quick adjustments as needed. His improved knowledge of the sport enables him to take advantage of opportunities and control his energy during fights.

To sum up, Francis Ngannou's fighting style combines powerful strikes, better footwork, and improved grappling techniques. Because of his commitment to development and adaptation, he can compete at the highest level in the heavyweight class thanks to his training program. Ngannou can now end bouts with deadly accuracy, cementing his place as one of the most dangerous competitors in MMA history.

Physical Attributes and Strength

A big part of Francis Ngannou's success as a mixed martial artist comes from his physical characteristics. Ngannou, who weighs over 250 pounds and is 6 feet 4 inches tall, stands out in the heavyweight class thanks to his combination of size, strength, and athleticism. His physique is the consequence of years of rigorous training and commitment to his job rather than just a hereditary trait.

Height and Reach

Ngannou has one of the longest reach lengths in the heavyweight class at 83 inches. This quality enables him to stay a safe distance from his opponents while still hitting them hard. Because of his height and reach advantage, he can use a range of striking methods, making it impossible for opponents to get closer without taking a risk from his potent blows. Ngannou's physical advantage is especially useful in stand-up sparring, as it allows him to land big strikes while keeping opponents at a distance.

Power Explosion

Ngannou is regarded as one of the most powerful strikers in MMA history. His combination of speed, technique, and muscle mass produces his explosive force. Because of his training regimen's emphasis on explosive movements, Ngannou can produce a great deal of force when striking. Several knockouts have resulted from this ability, which frequently ends contests with a single blow. His ability to use such force in the heavyweight class gives him a psychological advantage over opponents, who are aware of his capacity to stop fights quickly. This makes him a dangerous opponent.

Power and Conditioning

Ngannou's intense strength and conditioning regimen complements his athletic prowess. He performs a range of activities meant to improve his overall agility, endurance, and explosiveness. Important elements of his regimen include weightlifting, plyometrics, and functional training, which help him sustain high-performance levels and take hits during the fight. His training enables him to use strong blows to good effect even in the closing stages of a fight.

innate athleticism

Apart from his immense bulk and power, Ngannou has exceptional innate athleticism. For a man of his size, his remarkable quickness and agility allow him to maneuver around the octagon with ease. Because of his quickness, he can avoid blows and keep his equilibrium during battles, making him a challenging opponent to deal with. Ngannou's agility is further demonstrated by his ability to switch between striking and grappling, which enables him to adjust to various fighting situations with ease.

Sturdiness and Adaptability

Ngannou possesses a noteworthy degree of resilience and durability as well. He can take hits and bounce back fast because his physique is well-conditioned to resist the demands of mixed martial arts. In high-stakes battles, where the capacity to withstand damage frequently determines the result, this tenacity has been crucial. Together with his athletic prowess, Ngannou's mental toughness has proven essential to his capacity to overcome hardship and triumph.

In summary

In conclusion, Francis Ngannou's physical characteristics—such as his height, reach, strength, explosive power, and inherent athleticism—have a major role in his performance as a heavyweight fighter. These elements, together with his intense conditioning and training program, make him one of the most formidable mixed martial arts competitors. Ngannou is still a dominant force in the heavyweight class, frightening opponents and thrilling spectators everywhere as he honed his abilities and utilized his physical gifts.

Key Techniques and Knockouts

Francis Ngannou is one of the most feared knockout artists in mixed martial arts (MMA) thanks to his combination of strong hitting, efficient technique, and a developing skill set. His reputation as a top contender in the heavyweight class has been cemented by his lethal precision in finishing fights. The following crucial moves and noteworthy knockouts highlight Ngannou's aggressive fighting style:

Important Methods

Power Strikes: Ngannou's main weapons are strong hooks and crosses. He is renowned for having amazing knockout power. His left hook is especially deadly; when it connects squarely with an opponent's chin, it frequently results in an instant knockout. Ngannou possesses excellent footwork and body mechanics that enable him to transfer weight efficiently during strikes, which amplifies his punching power.

Overhand Right: Another one of Ngannou's hallmark movies is the overhand right. He frequently uses this blow to surprise opponents, particularly when they're trying to get closer. His overhand right is a deadly element in his striking arsenal since it can provide knockout power from unexpected angles.

Knees and Elbows: Ngannou uses his knees and elbows in close-quarters combat in addition to his punches. He can deal a lot of harm with these moves when opponents try to grapple or clinch with him. In tight circumstances, Ngannou's knee strikes in particular are useful for delivering fast, forceful punches to an opponent's head or torso.

Footwork & Angles: Ngannou's enhanced footwork enables him to sidestep oncoming blows and form angles for his strikes. He creates space with his lateral movement to avoid getting cornered and to set himself up for his power punches. This tactic gives him opportunities to deliver big hits and makes it tough for opponents to predict his next move.

Takedown Defense: Ngannou's primary position is striker, but he also possesses strong takedown defense abilities. He can make full use of his striking advantages since he can hold battles to a standstill. He practices guarding against takedowns with both legs and single legs, demonstrating his development as a complete fighter.

Notable Losses

Alistair Overeem (UFC on Fox 23): In December 2017, Ngannou scored one of his most memorable knockout victories against Alistair Overeem. Ngannou won the Performance of the Night bonus when, in the closing moments of the opening round, he delivered a stunning uppercut that knocked Overeem to the ground. Ngannou's career was defined by this knockout, which displayed his lightning-fast speed and timing.

Cain Velasquez (UFC on ESPN 1): In February 2019, Ngannou squared off against the former heavyweight champion, and the bout came to an explosive conclusion. With a strong right hand, Ngannou knocked out Velasquez in just 26 seconds, showcasing his striking ability and solidifying his place among the division's elite fighters.

Jairzinho Rozenstruik (UFC 249): Ngannou took on Rozenstruik in May 2020 and quickly dispatched him, finishing the fight in just 20 seconds. With one of the fastest finishes in UFC heavyweight history, Ngannou's clean left hook finish put an immediate stop to the bout, showcasing his speed and accuracy.

Stipe Miocic (UFC 260): Ngannou's career-defining rematch with Stipe Miocic at UFC 260 resulted in him winning the UFC Heavyweight Championship. Ngannou dominated Miocic with a strong left hook and then applied ground and pound in the second round, demonstrating both his development as a fighter and his capacity to end a top opponent with force.

Kurtis Blaydes (UFC Fight Night 141): Ngannou defeated Curtis Blaydes with a vicious uppercut in their rematch in November 2018, taking him to the canvas in just forty-five seconds. This victory showed off Ngannou's improved technical abilities and his capacity to perform well under duress in addition to his striking strength.

In summary

Francis Ngannou's explosive fighting style and development as a mixed martial artist are reflected in his signature moves and knockout victories. His enhanced talents in several MMA techniques together with his destructive strike output have made him a fearsome force in the heavyweight class. Ngannou continues to be an exciting fighter to watch, enthralling audiences with each explosive performance as he honed his skills and faced off against elite opponents.

Training Regimen and Work Ethic

Francis Ngannou's dedication to his craft and rigorous training program are major factors in his success in mixed martial arts (MMA). Recognizing the difficulties of the heavyweight class and the value of having a well-rounded skill set, Ngannou has dedicated himself to intense training and ongoing development. This is a synopsis of his training program and his guiding work ethic.

Exercise Plans

Training in Strikes: Ngannou spends a lot of time refining his striking techniques, which form the basis of his fighting philosophy. Among his impressive training are:

Pad Work: Practicing concentration mitts with coaches to improve speed, combinations, and technique.

Heavy Bag Work: Punching out loudly to build stamina and practice strong strikes.

Sparring: Practicing controlled sparring with different partners to imitate combat situations and hone his defensive, timing, and distance management abilities.

Grabbing and wrestling:

Ngannou has dedicated a lot of time to Brazilian Jiu-Jitsu and wrestling because he understands the significance of grappling in mixed martial arts. Among his training are:

Wrestling Drills: He can hone his grappling techniques by practicing escapes, takedown defense, and positional control.

Grappling Sparring: Practice ground exchanges and submissions by rolling with knowledgeable grapplers.

Strength and Conditioning: Ngannou aims to improve his general agility, explosive power, and endurance with a strength and conditioning regimen. Important elements consist of:

Weightlifting: To gain muscle and strength, concentrate on complex exercises like squats, deadlifts, and bench presses.

Plyometrics: Including explosive workouts that increase power output, such as medicine ball throws and box jumps.

Exercises that mimic combat intensity, or high-intensity interval training (HIIT), are a good way to increase cardiovascular endurance.

Mental Conditioning: Understanding the psychological difficulties associated with combat, Ngannou lays a strong focus on mental preparation. Among his mental training are:

Visualization Techniques: Using mental images to improve concentration and boost self-assurance before battles.

Stress management and maintaining composure under duress can be achieved by applying mindfulness practices.

Nutrition and Recuperation: A key component of Ngannou's training program is recuperation. His priorities are:

Days of rest: Letting his body recuperate after strenuous training sessions.

Massage therapy: This approach relieves tired muscles and helps people avoid injuries by combining massage and physical therapy.

Nutrition: Eating a well-balanced diet to support muscular growth and recuperation, with an emphasis on lean proteins, complex carbohydrates, and healthy fats. This diet feeds his workouts.

Workplace Morality

One of the things that sets Ngannou apart in his MMA style is his work ethic. He is the epitome of commitment, self-control, and an unwavering quest for growth. Important facets of his work ethic consist of:

Ngannou trains often, frequently spending a lot of time in the gym. His dedication to regular training sessions shows that he wants to improve his abilities and maintain his competitiveness.

Adaptability: Ngannou is willing to pick up new skills and tactics since he understands that a fighter must change over time. He customizes his training program to strengthen his areas of weakness and improve his strengths in close collaboration with trainers and sparring partners.

Resilience: Ngannou's experience of rising from poverty to success in the UFC has given him a strong feeling of fortitude. He views obstacles and failures as chances for development and uses them as fuel to push himself further.

Goal-oriented: Throughout preparation and competition, Ngannou establishes clear, quantifiable objectives for himself. He concentrates on reaching goals that are consistent with his long-term objectives, like winning the heavyweight title.

Inspiration to Others: Those who are enduring difficulty, in particular, find inspiration in Ngannou's work ethic and journey. Fans and aspiring fighters find inspiration in his tale of overcoming adversity, which inspires them to keep going after their goals despite difficulties.

In summary

The secret to Francis Ngannou's success as a mixed martial artist is his training schedule and work ethic. Ngannou continually improves as a fighter by using a thorough strategy that incorporates hitting, wrestling, training, and mental toughness. He is a strong opponent in the heavyweight division and a role model for aspiring athletes due to his passion and resilience, which show his commitment to greatness. Ngannou is still an exciting fighter to watch as he trains and gets better, enthralling spectators with every octagon performance.

Chapter 7: Challenges and Setbacks

Francis Ngannou had many obstacles and disappointments along the way to becoming a mixed martial arts (MMA) champion. Every challenge he overcame shaped his character and fortitude, making him the fighter he is today. The following are some of the main obstacles and disappointments that Ngannou faced during his career:

1. Early Life Difficulties

Ngannou experienced a difficult and impoverished upbringing in Cameroon. He had several difficulties as a child growing up in a tiny village, such as restricted access to opportunities and resources. Due to his family's financial difficulties and the fact that he frequently had to work to support them, he found it challenging to pursue athletics. Although this early misfortune gave him a strong work ethic, it also put obstacles in the way of his aspirations to be an athlete.

2. Immigration to Europe

There were difficulties associated with Ngannou's choice to leave Cameroon in pursuit of a better life. The harsh weather and crossing of the Sahara Desert were part of the arduous trek to Europe. He was homeless when he got to France and had a hard time adjusting to the new language and culture. His perseverance was put to the test, and he was forced to face the harsh realities of life as a migrant.

3. Getting Used to Parisian Life

After arriving in Paris, Ngannou had to deal with homelessness while pursuing his love of martial arts. He battled to find consistent training opportunities while living in shelters. He was nevertheless determined to practice mixed martial arts (MMA) and looked for clubs where he could advance his skills despite these challenges. He frequently struggled to acquire resources for training, food, and shelter, but his tenacity helped him stay focused on his objectives.

4. Early Career Setbacks

Ngannou experienced losses when he first started competing in mixed martial arts. He experienced setbacks early in his career that put his confidence to the test and made him rethink how he approached the game. These setbacks were instructive in that they showed him where he needed to develop. Ngannou did not let failures stop him; on the contrary, they gave him more drive to practice and improve.

5. Loss of the title shot

Ngannou suffered a severe defeat in his maiden championship defense against Stipe Miocic at UFC 220 in January 2018. A crucial turning point in his career occurred when he was unanimously declared the loser of the bout. This defeat made Ngannou's shortcomings clear and made him reevaluate his preparation and approach. Instead of giving in to discouragement, he focused on growing and becoming a more complete combatant by using the experience as fuel.

6. Expectations and Pressure

Ngannou encountered increasing demands and expectations from supporters and the media as he rose to prominence in the UFC. Being a title challenger carries a lot of responsibility, and Ngannou had to deal with the psychological effects of that. It took mental toughness and resilience to control expectations while concentrating on his training and performance.

7. Injury Difficulties

Ngannou has struggled with injuries throughout his career, which has prevented him from practicing and competing for periods of time. These wounds had an impact on his emotional health in addition to his physical readiness. Any athlete can be intimidated by the uncertainty of their recovery and the fear of losing their momentum, but Ngannou's perseverance allowed him to go beyond these obstacles and come back to the octagon stronger than before.

8. Handling Business and Contractual Decisions

Ngannou faced difficulties with contract negotiations and commercial decisions within the UFC as he gained notoriety. His career was further complicated by the intricacies of fight contracts, wage conflicts, and promotional considerations. He demonstrated his maturity as a combatant and businessman by carefully considering and taking a smart approach to navigating these challenges.

In summary

Francis Ngannou's life has been filled with many hardships and disappointments, ranging from his challenging childhood in Cameroon to the difficulties he encountered as a migrant and professional boxer. His perseverance, fortitude, and athletic development have all been enhanced by these challenges. Instead of letting failures define him, Ngannou has risen above them all to become one of the most formidable heavyweight champions in mixed martial arts history by using them as stepping stones to success. Many people find inspiration in his narrative, which highlights the value of tenacity and the capacity to overcome obstacles in the path of one's goals.

Losses and Learning Experiences

Any athlete's journey will always include setbacks, and for Francis Ngannou, each setback has had a significant impact on his character and career. Ngannou has accepted these obstacles as important teaching moments that have aided in his development as a fighter rather than letting them derail him. Below are a few significant setbacks in Ngannou's career along with the lessons he learnt from them:

1. UFC 220 loss against Stipe Miocic

In January 2018, Ngannou faced off against Stipe Miocic, who was the champion at the time. Ngannou was a clear favorite going into the bout, but after being outwitted and outclassed for five rounds, he was defeated by a unanimous decision. This loss exposed several crucial areas in which he still has to develop, such as his grappling defense, fight IQ, and ability to adjust to a more skilled opponent. Ngannou didn't let this defeat depress him; instead, he used it as motivation to improve his abilities and realize how crucial strategy is in the octagon.

2. UFC 226 loss vs Derrick Lewis

In a much-awaited fight, Ngannou took on Derrick Lewis in July 2018. Ngannou suffered a heartbreaking unanimous decision loss in the bout because neither boxer had any initiative and neither moved. For Ngannou, this bout was a turning point because it became clear how mental combat works and how crucial it is to remain calm under duress. Even in high-stakes scenarios, Ngannou discovered how important it is to keep his emotions in check and concentrate on his strategy.

3. Adjusting Following Failures

Ngannou changed his training regimen significantly after these defeats. In order to balance his striking ability, he focused on grappling and wrestling after seeing the necessity for a more diverse skill set. He emphasized the value of constant adaptation and progress by seeking advice from elite coaches and training partners. In addition to improving his technical skills, this practice strengthened his mental toughness, enabling him to go into subsequent fights more prepared and confident.

4. Fostering Mental Hardiness

Through his experiences, Ngannou learned the value of mental toughness in combat sports. Gaining the ability to overcome setbacks and see them as chances for improvement proved crucial to his progress as a fighter. He changed his perspective to one of optimism, utilizing his previous setbacks as fuel to work even harder in the gym and aim for perfection in all facets of his performance.

5. Accepting the Trip

Ngannou's disappointments gave him a greater understanding of the journey each athlete takes. He understood that losses are essential elements of the process rather than merely failures. He was able to approach every battle with a fresh outlook because of this mental shift, concentrating on the lessons he had learned rather than wallowing in his mistakes from the past.

6. Creating a More Robust Support Network

Ngannou also discovered the value of surrounding himself with a group of people who are encouraging. Following his defeats, he looked for mentors, training partners, and coaches with a wealth of expertise to help and support him. His comeback in the heavyweight class was largely attributed to this network, which was important in giving him his confidence back and helping him refocus his efforts.

In summary

The setbacks Francis Ngannou suffered and the lessons he learned from them helped to mold him into the warrior he is today. Every failure taught him something important, and those lessons shaped his training, attitude, and overall game plan. Ngannou's professional trajectory has been modified by embracing hardship and focussing on continual growth, which has ultimately led to his triumph as the UFC Heavyweight Champion. His story offers a reference to the strength of flexibility and tenacity as well as the significance of seeing setbacks as chances for personal development in the quest for greatness.

Overcoming Personal and Professional Obstacles

Francis Ngannou had numerous challenges in his personal and professional life that tested his fortitude, tenacity, and moral fiber before he emerged victorious as the UFC Heavyweight Champion. Ngannou has surmounted these obstacles and come out stronger as a result of her dedication and hard work, inspiring countless people in the process. Here's a closer look at the challenges he encountered and his strategy for overcoming them:

Individual Challenges

Poverty and Upbringing: Ngannou was raised in a modest home and had severe financial hardships as a young child. He was born in Cameroon. His lack of access to fundamental resources as a child growing up in a low-income family may have hampered his ability to pursue his sports goals. Ngannou used his background as inspiration rather than giving in to his situation. He put a lot of effort into providing for his family while pursuing his athletic goals, showing that perseverance can overcome adversity.

Migrant Struggles: Ngannou braved the dangerous trek to Europe, which required crossing the Sahara Desert and braving severe conditions, after deciding to leave Cameroon in search of a better life. He faced difficulties adjusting to French culture, language, and homelessness after his arrival. Although he could have easily given up after these encounters, Ngannou's persistence kept him going. He looked for neighborhood fitness centers, engrossing himself in mixed martial arts, and progressively starting over in Paris.

Mental Health Challenges: Ngannou's mental health suffered as a result of the strain of being a migrant and the uncertainties that came with starting a new life in Europe. He struggled with the tension between his dreams and reality at times, experiencing periods of terror and uncertainty. Nonetheless, Ngannou discovered a way to manage these psychological difficulties by concentrating on his objectives and surrounding himself with a community of support. He engaged in mindfulness and visualization exercises, which supported his resilience and mental clarity in the face of difficulty.

Obstacles in the workplace

Early Career Setbacks: Ngannou faced several difficulties throughout his first professional MMA venture. In the early stages of his career, he lost against Derrick Lewis and Stipe Miocic among other tough opponents. Although depressing, these mistakes proved to be important teaching moments. Ngannou transformed these setbacks into learning experiences by carefully examining his performance, addressing his areas of weakness, and modifying his training schedule.

Getting Started in the UFC and Getting Recognised: Ngannou had to deal with the difficulties of breaking into the promotion and negotiating contracts, not to mention the pressure of being a championship candidate. Ngannou discovered that while the demands of the public and fans could be daunting, he needed to concentrate on his preparation and octagon performance. To maintain focus on his objectives, he created a strategic approach to career management and sought advice from mentors.

Injury Difficulties: Ngannou experienced injury difficulties during his career, which occasionally prevented him from competing and training. These failures tried his mental fortitude in addition to his physical readiness. Ngannou didn't let injuries stop him from improving; instead, he made the most of the time to hone his abilities, become in better shape, and gain a better knowledge of the game. He showed resilience and an unwavering will to get back to his best performance by staying dedicated to his recuperation process.

Taking on Elite Competition: There were unique difficulties while taking on elite competitors in the heavyweight class. Ngannou discovered that every battle presents an opportunity for improvement and that he should approach each one with humility and respect for his opponents. He has been able to improve and succeed in the face of intense competition by researching his rivals and modifying his training to meet certain difficulties.

In summary

Francis Ngannou's journey serves as an example of the ability of tenacity to overcome setbacks in one's personal and professional life. He has become a fearsome champion due to his ability to overcome obstacles like poverty, migration, mental health issues, and the competitive world of mixed martial arts. Numerous people find inspiration in Ngannou's narrative, which shows that anyone can overcome any challenge on their way to realizing their dreams if they have perseverance, resilience, and an open mind. His story serves as a potent reminder that greatness is not only attained via triumphs but also with the bravery to persevere in the face of hardship and pursue greatness.

Chapter 8: Life Outside the Octagon

Though Francis Ngannou is most recognized for his electrifying exploits in the octagon, his background outside of mixed martial arts shows a complex person committed to changing the world for the better. Ngannou's life outside the cage demonstrates his character and dedication to self-improvement and community involvement, from his charitable endeavors to his hobbies outside of combat.

1. Charity and Involvement in the Community

Giving back to his community, especially in Cameroon, has become a top concern for Ngannou. He is committed to changing things since he is aware of the difficulties that many people in his own nation experience. His charitable endeavors consist of:

Support for Youth Sports: Ngannou has made investments in sports initiatives that give young people in Cameroon the chance to practice sports and advance their abilities. He thinks that sports have the ability to uplift young people and spur constructive change.

Charitable Donations: Ngannou has raised money for several causes, such as healthcare, education, and disaster relief operations in Cameroon, by using his platform. He has coordinated activities and worked with groups to direct funds toward initiatives that help the underprivileged.

2. Supporting the Rights of Migrants

Ngannou is passionate about promoting the rights of migrants and refugees since she has firsthand experience with the difficulties associated with migrating. He tells his tale to bring attention to the difficulties that many people encounter in their quest for a better life. Because of his experiences, Ngannou speaks out against injustices and supports programs that foster compassion and understanding for migrants.

3. Establishing a Name

Ngannou is concentrating on establishing his brand as an athlete and businessman in addition to competing. He engages in several commercial endeavors, such as endorsements and the selling of items. His goal is to leave a lasting legacy by using his platform to motivate and inspire upcoming generations, even after his fighting career is over.

4. Hobbies and Personal Interests

Ngannou likes to pursue hobbies outside of training and combat that help him have a healthy balance in his life. These include:

Ngannou has a strong interest in wellness and physical fitness. He frequently encourages his supporters to prioritize their physical and emotional well-being by sharing his training regimens and advice on leading a healthy lifestyle.

Travel and Exploration: Ngannou takes pleasure in seeing the world and learning about other cultures. His travels have given him the chance to interact with followers worldwide and gain knowledge from other societies.

Ngannou places a high importance on his friendships and family ties, frequently thanking them for their assistance over the years. Aside from battling, he cherishes the time he gets to spend with his loved ones and building relationships.

5. Motivating the Upcoming Generation

Ngannou tries to motivate young sportsmen and people going through difficult times by taking his responsibility as a public figure seriously. He interacts with followers on social media regularly, offering inspirational sayings and life lessons on tenacity and diligence. He hopes to inspire others to follow their aspirations despite all the challenges they may encounter by being transparent about his setbacks and victories.

6. Goals for the Future

Ngannou has stated that he hopes to have a greater influence outside of the octagon in the future. In addition to teaching and mentoring, he hopes to pursue career prospects in television or films, where he can spread his message of inspiration and representation. His objective is to use his MMA success to advocate for humanitarian causes and support charities that he believes in, changing the world for the better.

In summary

Francis Ngannou's life outside of the octagon demonstrates his dedication to advocacy, philanthropy, and personal development. Although he is well-known for his mixed martial arts accomplishments, his pursuits outside of the ring show a motivated and kind person who is committed to improving the lives of others. Through his charitable endeavors, support of immigrant rights, and attempts to uplift the younger generation, Ngannou is leaving a lasting legacy that goes well beyond the prison. His narrative serves as a potent reminder that genuine success is determined by one's influence on society at large as well as one's accomplishments.

Humanitarian Efforts

In addition to being incredible in the realm of athletics, Francis Ngannou's journey from a small Cameroonian town to the UFC Heavyweight Championship also serves as an inspirational tale of kindness and giving back. Since he is aware of the hardships that many people experience both at home and abroad, Ngannou has devoted his life to several humanitarian projects that try to enhance the lives of those who are less fortunate. A closer look at a few of his noteworthy humanitarian endeavors is provided below:

1. Assistance for the Youth of Cameroon

Ngannou is devoted to giving his native country's youth more power. He thinks that prospects for a better future and the shaping of young lives can be achieved through athletics. Among his initiatives are:

Sponsoring Local Sports Initiatives: Ngannou has made investments in regional sports programs that give young athletes access to resources and training. He hopes to encourage the next generation to follow their aspirations in athletics, just as he did, by contributing to youth initiatives.

Mentoring: Ngannou actively interacts with young athletes, providing them with career advice and mentoring. He talks about his experiences to inspire and encourage others to overcome obstacles and have faith in their abilities.

2. Charitable Contributions

Ngannou has raised money for several humanitarian initiatives, with a focus on health, education, and disaster assistance, utilizing his platform:

Education Initiatives: Ngannou has backed programs that give scholarships and educational materials to children in Cameroon, understanding the value of education in ending the cycle of poverty. He is aware that having access to a top-notch education can lead to positive changes that last a lifetime.

Support for Healthcare: Ngannou has partnered with institutions to offer healthcare to underserved communities. Raising money for those who cannot afford medical supplies and services is part of this.

3. Supporting the Rights of Migrants

Ngannou is enthusiastic about promoting the rights of migrants and refugees because he was once one of them. He has told his tale to bring attention to the difficulties that those who are trying to improve their lives face:

Increasing Awareness: Ngannou takes advantage of his position to draw attention to the challenges and tenacity faced by migrants. His goal in raising awareness of social concerns is to encourage compassion and understanding in society.

Support for Refugees: Ngannou works with groups that aid in the provision of resources and aid to people who have been uprooted due to violence or misfortune.

4. Involvement with the Community

Ngannou recognizes the value of contributing back to his society and becoming involved:

Local Outreach Initiatives: He takes part in outreach initiatives and community events that help and elevate marginalized groups. For people who look up to him as a role model, his presence frequently inspires and gives hope.

Fundraising Events: To support different philanthropic organizations, Ngannou plans and takes part in fundraising events. He frequently leverages his notoriety to bring resources and attention to significant concerns.

5. Creating a Legacy of Giving Ngannou wants to make a lasting contribution to society even after his MMA career is over, as seen by his humanitarian work. In the future, he hopes to expand his charitable endeavors and maybe start his foundation that would help young people and improve health and education in impoverished areas.

In summary

Francis Ngannou's humanitarian endeavors serve as evidence of his dedication to changing the world for the better. He has inspired and given hope to millions through his support of youth sports programs, charity endeavors, and advocacy for migrant rights. The life of Ngannou serves as a reminder that genuine success is determined by one's influence on other people as well as one's own accomplishments. Through his constant efforts, he leaves a lasting legacy that extends beyond the octagon uplifts communities, and empowers individuals.

Motivational Speeches and Public Appearances

Francis Ngannou's ascent to prominence as the UFC Heavyweight Champion is attributed to both his exceptional combat prowess and his capacity to uplift others via inspirational speeches and public appearances. His life story, which began in poverty in Cameroon and ended in success in mixed martial arts, is a stirring example of resiliency, willpower, and chasing one's aspirations. Ngannou wants to use his engagements to tell his narrative, inspire people to overcome obstacles and advocate good change. Here's a closer look at his attempts to motivate:

1. Explaining His Experience

During public appearances, Ngannou frequently recounts his amazing life story, highlighting the challenges he encountered and the tenacity needed to succeed. He engages listeners on a human level by openly sharing his experiences, inspiring them to follow their aspirations despite setbacks. His tale emphasizes that one's past does not dictate one's future and is especially relatable to individuals going through difficult times.

2. Motivational Orations

Ngannou has given inspirational talks at a range of occasions, such as community meetings, sports events, and schools. His talks frequently center on:

Overcoming Adversity: Ngannou places a strong emphasis on the value of resilience and keeping an optimistic outlook when dealing with difficulties. He uses personal tales to demonstrate how perseverance may pay off.

The Power of Dreams: He exhorts listeners to have faith in their goals and to work towards them tenaciously despite obstacles or social norms. Young athletes and aspirants who might be demoralized by their situation can relate to his message.

Hard Work and Dedication: According to Ngannou, achieving success takes dedication, discipline, and hard work; none of these things come easily. He frequently talks about his training schedule and the sacrifices he made to become the best in his field.

3. Interacting with Young People

Recognizing the importance of motivating the future generation, Ngannou actively interacts with young people by going on school visits, holding seminars, and hosting community events.

Mentoring: He provides advice and encouragement to young athletes in his capacity as a mentor. He inspires students to pursue greatness in their endeavors and maintain focus on their objectives by sharing his experiences.

Sports Clinics: Ngannou teaches important life lessons in addition to technical skills during sports clinics and training camps. Young sportsmen and wannabe warriors alike find motivation in his presence.

4. Media Presence

Ngannou has used these venues to reach wider audiences by appearing on several podcasts, television shows, and interviews:

Encouraging Positive Messages: He talks about the value of tenacity, mental toughness, and the ability to believe in oneself in interviews. His messages are compelling and accessible since they are frequently put within the framework of his personal story.

Advocacy for Social Issues: Ngannou makes use of his position to promote causes that are important to him, such as support for impoverished communities and migrant rights.

His dedication to social justice strikes a chord with many people, which increases his impact.

5. Establishing a Relationship with Fans

Ngannou cherishes his relationship with his followers and frequently interacts with them on social media, offering inspirational sayings and wisdom:

Encouragement: He creates a community of support by sharing content daily that encourages his followers to overcome obstacles and follow their aspirations.

Live Events and Q&A Sessions: Ngannou engages with fans directly by taking part in live events and Q&A sessions. He makes the most of these chances to tell his experience, respond to inquiries, and provide support.

In summary

Beyond the world of sports, Francis Ngannou's inspirational speeches and public appearances provide hope to people going through difficult times in all facets of life. His engaging narrative, social problem activism, and interactions with young people inspire others to embrace change, follow their ambitions, and have faith in the potential for positive transformation. Ngannou's dedication to empowering others exemplifies the enormous influence one person can have and shows that real greatness comes from having the capacity to uplift and inspire those around us in addition to achieving personal success.

Role Model and Inspiration

Francis Ngannou has become a highly regarded role model and inspiration to a great number of people, surpassing the realm of mixed martial arts (MMA) through his incredible journey and constructive influence on society. His life narrative, which is marked by tenacity, willpower, and a dedication to giving back, inspires and motivates people from a variety of backgrounds, making him a symbol of hope. Here are some more examples of how Ngannou inspires and acts as a role model:

1. Overcoming Misery

Ngannou's life story is one of overcoming hardship. He overcame many obstacles as a child, including homelessness and the hardships of migration, while living in poverty in Cameroon. His success in overcoming these obstacles is evidence of the value of tenacity. Ngannou's story shows that success is achievable regardless of one's upbringing or situation, encouraging people to face their obstacles head-on with bravery and tenacity.

2. Dream Pursuit

Ngannou is a living example of the idea of never giving up on your aspirations. His journey from a difficult upbringing to the title of UFC Heavyweight Champion shows that remarkable accomplishments may result from perseverance and hard effort. He exhorts people to establish high standards for themselves and put in great effort to reach them, stressing the need to have confidence in oneself when facing challenges.

3. Promotion of Social Concerns

In addition to his achievements in the octagon, Ngannou utilizes his position to promote critical social causes like migrant rights and assistance for impoverished areas. He spreads awareness and motivates people to act by speaking out on these issues. His dedication to helping others serves as more evidence that success ought to be accompanied by a sense of obligation to support and raise others.

4. Mentoring and advising

Ngannou constantly interacts with prospective fighters and young athletes, acting as a mentor and advisor. He inspires people to be focused and dedicated to their goals by sharing his experiences and providing support. His mentoring shows the value of paying it forward by fostering in the next generation a sense of hope and motivation.

5. Sincerity and Lowliness

Ngannou is an even better role model because of his genuineness and humility. He builds a sincere relationship with his fans and followers by being transparent about his challenges and successes. Because of his relatability, he serves as an inspiration to others, showing that even very successful people may maintain their moral principles and sense of purpose.

6. Encouraging an optimistic outlook

Ngannou highlights the value of mental toughness and optimism in conquering obstacles. He frequently delivers inspirational speeches about perseverance, self-belief, and the value of keeping a positive outlook despite adversity. His emphasis on mental health inspires others to develop an outlook that promotes development and achievement.

7. Leaving a Trace

In addition to his accomplishments in mixed martial arts, Ngannou is dedicated to leaving a lasting legacy that will motivate the next generations. In his native country and abroad, he hopes to start foundations and programs that promote youth, education, and health. His drive to make a difference guarantees that his influence goes well beyond his professional boxing career.

In summary

Francis Ngannou's remarkable journey and steadfast dedication to changing the world are the foundation of his status as an inspiration to others. Numerous people are motivated to trust in themselves and aspire to greatness by his inspirational tale of overcoming adversity, pursuing aspirations, advocating for social causes, and commitment to mentoring. Ngannou is a relatable character who demonstrates that real strength comes from the capacity to empower and encourage others in addition to physical capability. His humility, genuineness, and positive outlook further solidify this point. Ngannou continues to change lives both within and outside of the octagon, serving as a symbol of optimism and a constant reminder of the value of giving back and the possibility of personal growth.

Chapter 9: Legacy and Future Prospects

Francis Ngannou has had a significant influence on the mixed martial arts (MMA) community and beyond. His legacy is being shaped by his accomplishments within the octagon as well as his attempts to encourage and uplift those outside of it. As he travels forward, Ngannou leaves behind a legacy of fortitude, generosity, and a strong desire to bring about change. A closer look at his legacy and potential goes here:

A New Chapter in MMA's Heavyweight Class
Ngannou's ascent to fame in the UFC has revolutionized the heavyweight class. His fast fighting style, which is characterized by remarkable athleticism and knockout power, has enthralled spectators and reignited interest in the game. Ngannou has paved the path for upcoming fighters by setting a new benchmark for excellence in mixed martial arts (MMA) by defeating famous opponents and winning the

heavyweight belt. Being one of the most formidable heavyweight champions in UFC history solidifies his legacy in the sport.

2. Motivating Next Generations

Aspiring fighters and others going through hardship can draw great inspiration from Ngannou's path from poverty to champion. His narrative inspires others to have faith in their abilities and to tenaciously follow their goals. His interactions with young sportsmen and the experiences he offers are helping to shape the next generation of fighters who look up to him. His dedication to mentoring and backing child sports programs solidifies his reputation as a source of inspiration for a great number of people.

3. Donations to Charities

Ngannou's charitable work is a significant part of his legacy. He is genuinely improving the lives of people in need by sponsoring young initiatives, speaking up on social concerns, and helping impoverished areas. His altruistic efforts emphasize the value of giving back, and the improvements he makes to the communities he supports will serve as a lasting testament to his legacy. Ngannou's commitment to philanthropy guarantees that his impact goes well beyond his professional wrestling career.

4. Supporting the Rights of Migrants

Ngannou is enthusiastic about defending the rights of people looking for a better life because she was herself a migrant. His candor in his experiences as a migrant helps to increase awareness of the difficulties many encounter. He is making a significant contribution to crucial discussions regarding immigration and human rights by leveraging his platform to promote social justice. This part of his legacy assures that a wider audience will be able to relate to his tale by positioning him as a voice for individuals who are frequently ignored.

5. Prospective Career Paths

Ngannou is not just investigating alternatives outside of combat but also developing as an athlete. Among his ambitions could be:

Coaching and Mentorship: Ngannou is probably going to think about helping to train and teach the upcoming fighters, passing along his skills and experiences to make them successful.

Media and Entertainment: Ngannou may pursue media opportunities, such as appearances in documentaries, interviews, and possibly acting, due to his captivating story and charisma. His genuineness and charm could be a great fit for these new opportunities.

Business ventures: Ngannou is now engaged in several business endeavors. He might look at starting new businesses that are in line with his hobbies, such as those involving sports, nutrition, and fitness gear.

6. Creating an Enduring Basis

Ngannou has stated that he wants to establish a foundation that will support young people and advance health and education in Cameroon and other countries. He hopes to leave a constructive legacy that will continue to influence future generations by founding such an organization.

In summary

The legacy of Francis Ngannou is complex and includes his contributions to philanthropy, his accomplishments in the octagon, and his advocacy for social change. Ngannou is well-positioned to carry on having a big influence in a lot of different areas in the future, like mentoring young athletes, advocating, and looking into new professional paths. His narrative serves as a reminder that greatness is defined by one's capacity to uplift others and bring about constructive change in the world, not by one's achievements. Ngannou's legacy will surely keep expanding and inspiring for years to come because of his uncompromising adherence to his principles and his enthusiasm for encouraging others around him.

What's Next for Francis Ngannou

Francis Ngannou has a bright future ahead of him, full of opportunities to mold his career and make a difference in the sports industry and beyond. Fans, pundits, and aspiring fighters will be keenly observing Ngannou's next moves after his stellar UFC career and noteworthy accomplishments as a heavyweight champion. A peek at what could come next for him is as follows:

Making the switch to boxing

A move to professional boxing is among Ngannou's most discussed options. Owing to his knockout prowess and striking ability, he has shown enthusiasm in taking on top boxers, possibly even in high-profile fights against seasoned veterans. This move can raise his status as a combat sports athlete and present him with new challenges as well as substantial cash gain prospects.

2. Ongoing Humanitarian Work and Advocacy

Ngannou is devoted to social justice activism and humanitarian activities, especially in the areas of migrant rights and aiding impoverished communities. He might concentrate more on these projects in the upcoming years, either starting his foundation or collaborating with already-existing organizations to have a significant effect. Many people can relate to his narrative of overcoming hardship, and he will probably keep utilizing his platform to encourage change.

3. Mentoring and Coaching

Given his extensive background and expertise in mixed martial arts, Ngannou might think about taking on a coaching or mentoring role. He could provide young fighters with guidance and support by offering advice on training, mentality, and negotiating the challenges of a professional fighting career. Through this change, he would be able to continue his connection to the sport he loves and inspire the athletes of tomorrow.

4. Opportunities for Media and Entertainment

Ngannou is a great contender for several media and entertainment projects due to his captivating tale and endearing demeanor. He might look for roles in films, TV shows, or documentaries, which could allow him to share his story with a larger audience. His future may potentially include writing a memoir, doing podcasts, or giving public speeches, which would enable him to inspire others and reach a larger audience.

5. Establishing a Portfolio for Your Business

Ngannou might investigate entrepreneurial endeavors that coincide with his ideals and areas of interest as he looks to the future. This could be companies that cater to exercise enthusiasts, nutritional goods, or programs that support well-being and health. By utilizing his reputation and power, he might open doors that would benefit his community's well-being in addition to bringing him financial success.

6. Taking Part in Different Combat Sports

Ngannou may look into prospects in combat sports like kickboxing or bare-knuckle boxing in addition to boxing. His striking prowess and MMA background make him a versatile athlete with the ability to transition between various fighting techniques. Participating in a variety of forms could provide his profession excitement and lead to new opportunities.

7. Development and Personal Growth

Ngannou has stressed the value of ongoing development for both individuals and athletes. He might put more of an emphasis on training, bettering himself, and discovering interests outside of combat sports. This self-discovery path may present unforeseen chances and encounters.

In summary

There are a tonne of intriguing opportunities for Francis Ngannou's future that go beyond his professional fighting career. Whether Ngannou moves into boxing, broadens his humanitarian work, coaches up-and-coming athletes, or pursues media and commercial endeavors, his influence will probably never go away among both supporters and locals. His journey guarantees that, whichever route he takes, it will be one of significance and purpose. It also serves as a reminder of the strength of resilience and the ability to inspire others. Ngannou continues to be a source of inspiration and tenacity for aspirant fighters and people overcoming obstacles throughout the world as he begins this new chapter.

His Impact on the MMA World

Francis Ngannou has redefined expectations and inspired a new generation of competitors, leaving a lasting impression on the mixed martial arts (MMA) scene. In addition to being a monument to his skill and perseverance, his path from a difficult childhood in Cameroon to the title of UFC Heavyweight Champion also represents larger shifts in the sport. Taking a closer look at Ngannou's influence on the world of mixed martial arts

1. Defining the Division of Heavyweights

The intense fighting style and knockout power of Ngannou have reignited interest in the heavyweight class. His spectacular finish skills have raised the entertainment value of heavyweight matches and established new performance benchmarks. Fans' interest in heavyweight bouts has surged due to Ngannou's distinctive combination of power and athleticism, which has revived the division's popularity.

2. Motivational Underdogs

People who are enduring hardship and those who aspire to be fighters can relate to Ngannou's narrative. His journey from adversity and poverty to champion status is a stirring illustration of tenacity and fortitude. Through his candid sharing of his path and challenges, he encourages many people to follow their aspirations no matter what. Underdogs in all spheres of life are inspired by Ngannou's story to dream big and pursue achievement.

3. Improving African Fighters' Status

Due to Ngannou's popularity, the number of talented African mixed martial artists has increased. He set the path for other African fighters to achieve exposure and possibilities in the sport as one of the first African champions in the UFC. By inspiring additional fighters from the region to seek careers in the sport and demonstrating the amount of talent available, Ngannou's accomplishments help promote African mixed martial arts (MMA) on the global stage.

4. Promoting MMA Awareness Worldwide

Ngannou's accomplishments and voyage have helped MMA become a global sport. His narrative has attracted interest outside of the sport, reaching a variety of audiences and igniting a global passion for combat sports. As the sport's representative, he has contributed to de-mystifying MMA so that fans of different backgrounds may relate to and understand it better.

5. Encouraging Social Transformation

In addition to being an athlete, Ngannou is a social justice activist who supports impoverished areas and migrant rights in particular. Through the use of his platform, he has encouraged others in the MMA community to take up activism and philanthropy in response to these pressing issues. Fighters and sports organizations are encouraged to use their power for good by Ngannou's dedication to humanitarian causes.

6. Putting Traditional Fighting Styles to the Test

The conventional notions of heavyweight boxers are challenged by Ngannou's distinctive fighting technique. Acclaimed for his speed and hitting ability, he dispels the myth that heavyweight fighters are just fighters. His style blends power, speed, and technique to push the envelope for fighters in his weight class and encourage others to take up more dynamic fighting techniques.

7. Establishing a Business and Brand

The MMA business has been impacted by Ngannou's success as well. Fighters may take note of his example and seek more control over their careers as he develops his brand and pursues new chances. His switch to boxing and possible economic endeavors may open doors for other fighters to seek opportunities outside of their sport, expanding their horizons.

8. A Tradition of Excellence

Ngannou's dedication to perfection and his never-ending quest for development have established a benchmark for MMA competitors. Aspiring athletes can learn from his work ethic and commitment to training, which highlight the value of discipline and tenacity in reaching the pinnacles of competition.

In summary

Francis Ngannou has had a profound effect on the mixed martial arts community through his accomplishments in the ring, his position as an industry ambassador, and his dedication to social change. His story raises the profile of mixed martial arts (MMA) internationally, motivates a lot of people, and emphasizes the potential of African fighters. Ngannou's legacy will definitely have an impact on mixed martial arts for years to come as he continues to change the field and inspire us to follow our aspirations and be resilient.

Conclusion

Francis Ngannou's rise from modest origins in Cameroon to prominence in mixed martial arts is evidence of the strength of perseverance, diligence, and steadfast resolve. His influence on the sport goes beyond his remarkable physical accomplishments; it also includes his dedication to bringing about positive change in the world and his role as an example to innumerable others suffering from struggle.

Ngannou's explosive fighting style has revolutionized the heavyweight category, grabbing fans' interest and reviving the MMA scene. As a champion, he has improved the standing of African fighters and demonstrated the sport's attraction to a worldwide audience, encouraging a new generation of sportsmen to follow their goals in sports.

Beyond the octagon, Ngannou's commitment to having a significant influence is demonstrated by his support of social causes, especially those about immigrant rights and aiding impoverished areas. His readiness to give back to the community and share his experience serves as an example of the larger duty that comes with notoriety and success.

Ngannou's prospective career paths—boxing, coaching, and philanthropy—offer intriguing chances for ongoing development and impact as he looks to the future. His impact on people's lives and the positive transformation he inspires define his legacy more so than his championship victories.

Francis Ngannou is a source of optimism in a world that frequently appears to be full of difficulties. He demonstrates that everyone can achieve greatness and overcome hurdles if they have the will and heart to do so. His legacy will live on as people all over the world are inspired by his narrative to follow their passions and improve their local communities, guaranteeing that his influence on mixed martial arts and society will last for many more generations.

www.ingramcontent.com/pod-product-compliance
Lightning Source LLC
LaVergne TN
LVHW021446231224
799792LV00005B/409